Google Cloud AI Services Quick Start Guide

Build intelligent applications with Google Cloud AI services

Arvind Ravulavaru

BIRMINGHAM - MUMBAI

Google Cloud AI Services Quick Start Guide

Commissioning Editor: Amey Varangaonkar
Acquisition Editor: Reshma Raman
Content Development Editor: Aditi Gour
Technical Editor: Jinesh Topiwala
Copy Editor: Safis Editing
Project Coordinator: Hardik Bhinde
Proofreader: Safis Editing
Indexer: Tejal Daruwale Soni
Graphics: Jason Monteiro
Production Coordinator: Aparna Bhagat

First published: May 2018

Production reference: 1280518

Published by Packt Publishing Ltd.
Livery Place
35 Livery Street
Birmingham
B3 2PB, UK.

ISBN 978-1-78862-661-3

www.packtpub.com

To the end of Human race, powered by Artificial Intelligence.

`mapt.io`

Mapt is an online digital library that gives you full access to over 5,000 books and videos, as well as industry leading tools to help you plan your personal development and advance your career. For more information, please visit our website.

Why subscribe?

- Spend less time learning and more time coding with practical eBooks and Videos from over 4,000 industry professionals

- Improve your learning with Skill Plans built especially for you

- Get a free eBook or video every month

- Mapt is fully searchable

- Copy and paste, print, and bookmark content

PacktPub.com

Did you know that Packt offers eBook versions of every book published, with PDF and ePub files available? You can upgrade to the eBook version at `www.PacktPub.com` and as a print book customer, you are entitled to a discount on the eBook copy. Get in touch with us at `service@packtpub.com` for more details.

At `www.PacktPub.com`, you can also read a collection of free technical articles, sign up for a range of free newsletters, and receive exclusive discounts and offers on Packt books and eBooks.

Contributors

About the author

Arvind Ravulavaru is a platform architect at Ubiconn IoT Solutions, with over 9 years of experience in software development and 2 years in hardware and product development. For the last 5 years, he has been working extensively on JavaScript, both on the server side and the client side, and for the last couple of years he has working in IoT, building a platform for rapidly developing IoT solutions named The IoT Suitcase. Prior to that, Arvind worked on big data, cloud computing, and orchestration.

About the reviewer

Chirag Nayyar helps organizations initiate their digital transformation using the public cloud. He has been actively working on cloud platforms since 2013, providing consultancy to many organizations ranging from SMB to Enterprises. He holds a wide range of certifications from all major public cloud platforms. He also runs meetups and is a regular speaker at various cloud events. He has also reviewed *Hands-On Machine Learning on Google Cloud Platform* and *Google Cloud Platform Cookbook*, by Packt.

Packt is searching for authors like you

If you're interested in becoming an author for Packt, please visit authors.packtpub.com and apply today. We have worked with thousands of developers and tech professionals, just like you, to help them share their insight with the global tech community. You can make a general application, apply for a specific hot topic that we are recruiting an author for, or submit your own idea.

Table of Contents

Preface

Cognition as a Service (CAAS) is the new kid on the block. No longer do engineers need to spend time building intelligence on top of their applications. Now, intelligence is borrowed from various services.

Welcome to *Google Cloud AI Services Quick Start Guide*, where we will explore the powerful Google Cloud AI services via a project-based approach. We will build a forum application named *SmartExchange*, similar to Discourse or stack overflow, where users start a discussion thread and other users comment on it. To administer the content that goes into the *SmartExchange* application, we will use Google Cloud AI services such as the Cloud Vision API and Video Intelligence API.

Who this book is for

This book is ideal for any reader who would like to use the power of Google Cloud AI services in their projects without going through the pain of mastering machine learning for images, videos, and text. Any reader who would like to get acquainted with Cloud AI services provided by Google will also find this book interesting.

Readers need to have prior knowledge of working with REST API services and should have an idea of working with the *MEAN* application stack. Basic knowledge of TypeScript is also essential for successfully completing this book.

What this book covers

Chapter 1, *Introducing Google Cloud AI Services*, introduces you to the world of **Google Cloud Platform** (GCP). You will understand various services provided by GCP, and we will deep dive into all the services provided by Google Cloud AI services. You will understand the basics of machine learning and AI in this chapter and how they tie in with Cognition as a Service (CAAS).

Chapter 2, *Setting Up a Smart Forum App*, walks you through the architecture and design of the application (*SmartExchange*) we will build. We will understand the database schema and the application stack. We will then download the base application and set it up. We will also set up the required keys for accessing Google Cloud AI services.

Chapter 3, *Cloud Vision API*, explains how to work with the Cloud Vision API over REST API. We will explore various features that we can detect using this API. Finally, we will integrate the Cloud Vision API services with *SmartExchange*.

Chapter 4, *Video Intelligence API*, focuses on how to work with the Video Intelligence API over REST API. We will explore various features that we can detect using this API. Finally, we will integrate the Video Intelligence API services with *SmartExchange*.

Chapter 5, *Cloud Speech API*, looks at how to work with the Cloud Speech API over REST API. We will explore various features that we can detect using this API. Finally, we will integrate the Cloud Speech API with *SmartExchange*.

Chapter 6, *Cloud Natural Language*, outlines how to work with the Cloud Natural Language API over REST API. We will explore various features that we can detect using this API. Finally, we will integrate the Cloud Natural Language API with *SmartExchange*.

Chapter 7, *Cloud Translation*, explains how to work with the Cloud Translation API over REST API. We will explore how to translate a piece of text into other languages using this API. Finally, we will integrate the Cloud Translation API with *SmartExchange*.

To get the most out of this book

To work with the content of the book, you will need knowledge of the following technologies:

- MongoDB
- Node.js
- ExpressJS
- Mongoose
- Angular 5
- TypeScript
- REST API services

You need to have Node.js 6.13.1 installed on your machine to follow along with this book.

Download the example code files

You can download the example code files for this book from your account at `www.packtpub.com`. If you purchased this book elsewhere, you can visit `www.packtpub.com/support` and register to have the files emailed directly to you.

You can download the code files by following these steps:

1. Log in or register at `www.packtpub.com`.
2. Select the **SUPPORT** tab.
3. Click on **Code Downloads & Errata**.
4. Enter the name of the book in the **Search** box and follow the onscreen instructions.

Once the file is downloaded, please make sure that you unzip or extract the folder using the latest version of:

- WinRAR/7-Zip for Windows
- Zipeg/iZip/UnRarX for Mac
- 7-Zip/PeaZip for Linux

The code bundle for the book is also hosted on GitHub at `https://github.com/PacktPublishing/Google-Cloud-AI-Services Quick-Start-Guide`. In case there's an update to the code, it will be updated on the existing GitHub repository.

We also have other code bundles from our rich catalog of books and videos available at `https://github.com/PacktPublishing/`. Check them out!

Download the color images

We also provide a PDF file that has color images of the screenshots/diagrams used in this book. You can download it here: `https://www.packtpub.com/sites/default/files/downloads/GoogleCloudAIServicesQuickStartGuide_ColorImages.pdf`.

Code in Action

Visit the following link to check out videos of the code being run:

`https://goo.gl/cViHRf`.

Conventions used

There are a number of text conventions used throughout this book.

`CodeInText`: Indicates code words in text, database table names, folder names, filenames, file extensions, pathnames, dummy URLs, user input, and Twitter handles. Here is an example: "This will install all the dependencies listed. Next, open the entire application in your favorite editor, and then open `README.md`."

A block of code is set as follows:

```
//SNIPP SNIPP
{
     "inputContent": "/9j/7QBEUGhvdG9zaG9...base64-encoded-video-
content...fXNWzvDEeYxxxzj/Coa6Bax//Z",
     "features": ["LABEL_DETECTION"]
 }
//SNIPP SNIPP
```

Any command-line input or output is written as follows:

```
$ yarn add @google-cloud/video-intelligence
```

Bold: Indicates a new term, an important word, or words that you see onscreen. For example, words in menus or dialog boxes appear in the text like this. Here is an example: "Click on **New** and then **Request** inside Postman."

 Warnings or important notes appear like this.

 Tips and tricks appear like this.

Get in touch

Feedback from our readers is always welcome.

General feedback: Email feedback@packtpub.com and mention the book title in the subject of your message. If you have questions about any aspect of this book, please email us at questions@packtpub.com.

Errata: Although we have taken every care to ensure the accuracy of our content, mistakes do happen. If you have found a mistake in this book, we would be grateful if you would report this to us. Please visit www.packtpub.com/submit-errata, selecting your book, clicking on the Errata Submission Form link, and entering the details.

Piracy: If you come across any illegal copies of our works in any form on the Internet, we would be grateful if you would provide us with the location address or website name. Please contact us at copyright@packtpub.com with a link to the material.

If you are interested in becoming an author: If there is a topic that you have expertise in and you are interested in either writing or contributing to a book, please visit authors.packtpub.com.

Reviews

Please leave a review. Once you have read and used this book, why not leave a review on the site that you purchased it from? Potential readers can then see and use your unbiased opinion to make purchase decisions, we at Packt can understand what you think about our products, and our authors can see your feedback on their book. Thank you!

For more information about Packt, please visit packtpub.com.

Introducing Google Cloud AI Services

1

Cognition as a Service (**CAAS**) is the new kid on the block. No longer do engineers need to spend time building intelligence on top of their applications. Now, intelligence is borrowed from various services.

Welcome to *Google Cloud AI Services Quick Start Guide*, where we are going to explore the powerful Google Cloud AI services via a project-based approach. We are going to build a forum application named *SmartExchange*, similar to Discourse or Stack Overflow, where users start a discussion thread and other users comment on it.

To manage the content that goes into the *SmartExchange* application, we are going to use Google Cloud AI services such as Cloud Vision API and Video Intelligence API.

In this chapter, we are going to cover the following:

- What is Google Cloud Platform?
- Cognition in the cloud
- What is Google Cloud AI?
- Overview of Google Cloud AI services

Google Cloud Platform

We are going to start by understanding **Google Cloud Platform** (**GCP**). GCP is a collection of services that leverages the power of Cloud Computing (`https://azure.microsoft.com/en-in/overview/what-is-cloud-computing/`). Along with these services, GCP also offers tools to manage these services.

GCP has a command-line interface or Cloud SDK (`https://cloud.google.com/sdk/`), using which engineers can easily manage and monitor these services.

As of March 2018, GCP has the following verticals of services, which we will discuss in the following subsections. You can read more about Google Platform offerings here: `https://cloud.google.com/products/`.

Compute

Compute offers infrastructure to perform user-defined computing. Some of the services in this vertical are the **Compute Engine**, **App Engine**, and **Cloud Functions**.

Big data

As the name suggests, **Big data** provides tools needed to work with large volumes of data. Some of the services in this vertical are **BigQuery**, **Cloud Datalab**, and **Genomics**.

Identity and security

Identity and security provides tools needed for identity, access, and content security. Some of the services in this vertical are **Cloud IAM**, **Cloud Resource Manager**, and **Cloud Security Scanner**.

Internet of Things (IoT)

Currently, GCP has one core service, named **Cloud IoT Core**, under **Internet of Things (IoT)**, which provides device management services when working with IoT.

Storage and databases

Storage and databases provides storage services when dealing with large volumes of data. Right from object storage to block storage, this vertical has all the services needed. Some of the services in this vertical are cloud storage, **Cloud Bigtable**, **Cloud SQL**, **Cloud Spanner**, and **Persistent Disk**.

Data transfer

Data transfer services help us easily import or export data from one service to another. The three services currently in this vertical are **Google BigQuery Data Transfer Service, Cloud Storage Transfer Service**, and **Google Transfer Appliance**.

API platform and ecosystem

API platform and ecosystem offers services that help in managing and protecting APIs. From **API monetization** to API analytics, this vertical offers them all. This vertical also supports Apigee platform services.

Management tools

Management tools offers tools needed to manage various cloud services offered by GCP. This service has tools needed for logging, monitoring, and controlling various other GCP services.

Networking

Networking offers **Virtual Private Cloud (VPC)**, **Content Delivery Network (CDN)**, and **Domain-Naming Systems (DNS)**, to name a few.

Cloud AI

Cloud AI offers various services that are needed to add Artificial Intelligence to our applications. **Cloud-based machine learning, Cloud Vision API**, and **Cloud Speech API** are some of these services.

Developer tools

Last, but not the least, the developer tools provides all the essential tools developers need to quickly bring up an application or a solution on top of GCP. Some of the software under this offering includes container registry, **Cloud Test Lab, Cloud Tools for Eclipse**, and **Cloud SDK**.

In this book, we are going to work closely with the Cloud AI vertical. In the next section, we are going to look at the what and the why of Cloud AI.

Cognition on cloud

In the last section, we saw the various services offered by Google Cloud Platform. One of the services we saw in that section is Google Cloud AI Services. Before we start exploring Google Cloud AI Services, let's understand what it's importance is.

We have been using the cloud as a central entity for storing data and providing scalable computing for more than a decade now. Until recently, all applications had intelligence built in locally. Times have changed; we are now using the cloud as a central dispatcher for intelligence. We have separated the application from its intelligence and have hosted the intelligence so that everyone can use it and not just the application.

So, what exactly is AI in the cloud? It is when *clients* upload *data* to *a cognitive service,* and the service responds with a prediction.

Let's take a moment to understand the three previously highlighted terms: the clients, the data, and the cognitive service. This helps us better define AI on the cloud.

Clients

When I say clients, I mean any device that has the capability of making an HTTP request to an endpoint and being able to resolve the response.

This could be a simple web/mobile/desktop application or a piece of smart internet-enabled hardware such as an IoT device, a voice assistant, a smartwatch, or a smart camera.

If these were defined as clients, what would the data that we are dealing with be?

Data types

As we have seen the different types of clients, let's see what kinds of data they produce.

In today's world, data can be categorized into three types:

- **Structured data**: Structured data is well defined data and the entire dataset follows a schema for such data. Examples of structured data are CSV files and RDBMS databases.
- **Unstructured data**: Unstructured data, on the other hand, is not well defined and there are structural changes to the data throughout the dataset. Examples of unstructured data are audio files, video files, and image files.
- **Semi-structured data**: Data that is present in emails, log files, text files, or word documents is considered unstructured data.

So, data has three types, and we need a cognitive service that can consume this data and respond with an intelligent response. So, let's define what a cognitive service is.

Cognitive services

A cognitive service is a piece of computing software that can consume a data type that we have defined previously and respond with a cognitive response.

A simple example of a cognitive service is **image intelligence**. This is the ability to upload an image to view its contents and label it. Almost all of us have experienced this feature using the camera app, where the camera software can detect faces and detect smiles on those faces. This is image intelligence.

Another type of intelligence is **sentiment analysis**. Given a few paragraphs of text, the cognitive service can detect the emotions in the text. A simple example could be a product Twitter account feeding all the tweets it's tagged in into a cognitive service to see the overall sentiment of people using the product.

Of late, video intelligence has become even more common. This is the ability to scan a video's contents and label it for rapid detection of content in various frames and scenes, and this is very helpful for navigating and indexing a long video.

Now that we understand what AI on the cloud is, let's look at why we need it.

Why Cognition on Cloud?

This is a very important question that one needs to understand before going further. Here are a few reasons:

- Distributed global intelligence
- Process large volumes of data
- Process different types of data
- Cognitive accuracy

Distributed global intelligence defines how cognition as a service, when placed in a central location, can be used by many more entities to make them smart, rather than just one application.

Processing large volumes of data defines how the power of cloud computing can handle large volumes of data efficiently, which a normal computer or a human being would find difficult.

Processing different types of data defines how the cognitive service can process various types of data without much effort.

Cognitive accuracy is one of the most important features of all. The more data a machine learning algorithm service consumes, the better its accuracy. We will talk more about this in the next sections.

How do machines achieve intelligence?

Accuracy depends on how we train the system. There are two ways for machines to learn something:

- Rule-based learning
- Pattern-based learning

In rule-based learning, the developer defines a bunch of rules and the machine parses the incoming data against those rules to come to a conclusion. This approach is good for monotonous systems and where things do not change that often.

What if we are trying to build ;intelligence for a weather prediction system? Will the learning that we have had up to today be enough for us to get an accurate prediction, even after 50 years? Maybe not.

This is where pattern-based learning comes in. Pattern-based learning is more popularly known as **machine learning (ML)**. In today's world, most of the learning by computers happens through machine learning. Let's take a quick look at how ML plays an important role in this.

Cognitive accuracy and machine learning

Machine learning is the process a machine follows to learn about various things. Some things are easier to learn than others.

Artificial Intelligence is a collection of such machine learnings that can be put to use in the real world to make decisions or to predict something.

Here is a diagram that shows how a typical machine learns:

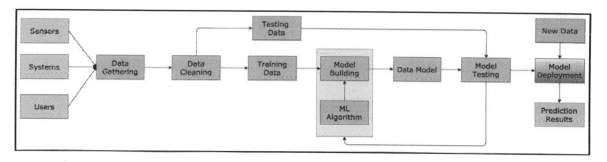

We have a data-gathering source at one end, which gets data from various reliable sources, depending on the solution. This data has both **features** and **labels**. Features are columns of data that are taken as input to learning, and labels are the expected outcome for that set of features. Let's take a look at an example of weather station data:

Temperature	Humidity	Wind	Rainfall
17 degrees Celsius	87%	5 km per hour	10 mm
23 degrees Celsius	23%	1 km per hour	0 mm

The columns named **Temperature**, **Humidity**, and **Wind** are features, and **Rainfall** is a label, in our table. Using this type of supervised learning, we would build a data model from this data and ask a question such as: Given the following features, what is the chance of rain?

The data we gather is the most important part of machine learning, as the quality and quantity of data define the accuracy of prediction.

Once the data has been gathered, this data is then cleaned and normalized. The cleaned data is then split into two parts, training data and testing data. Training data is used to train the data model and testing data is used to cross-validate the accuracy of the data model.

Now, depending on the type of cognitive service we want to provide, we would use a machine learning algorithm and feed the training data to it, building something called a data model.

A data model is a snapshot of the learning and this snapshot is now tested against the testing data. This step is critical in analyzing the accuracy of the data model.

The model can be trained again and again with various sets of data to have a better accuracy. Once the model is completed, we host it as an API for other systems to query it, passing their features. Based on the prediction results from here on, we would refine the data model.

The previous process is how most cognitive services are built. Now, one of the key steps of data model accuracy depends on the quality and quantity of data.

The more accurate the data that is fed to the machine learning algorithm, the higher the quality of the data model.

Imagine a cognitive service such as explicit image detection built by you or your organization. We need data to train this cognitive service to start with. How many images can we feed it, 1 million, 2 million? Imagine the size of infrastructure needed for training about 10 million images.

Once the service is built, how many hits will your users make? 1 million requests per day? And will this be sufficient to know the accuracy of your model and improve it?

Now, on the other hand, consider data models built by the likes of Google, which pretty much has access to almost all the content of the internet. And imagine the number of people using this service, thus helping the cognitive service to learn by experience.

Within no time, a cognitive service like this will be far more accurate, not only for mainstream scenarios, but also corner cases.

In cognitive services, accuracy increases with the quality and quantity of data and this is one of the main things that adds value to cloud-based cognition over local intelligence.

Take a look at this video titled *Inside Google Translate*: `https://www.youtube.com/watch?v=_GdSC1Z1Kzs`, which explains how the Google Translate service works. This re-emphasizes the thought I expressed previously about how machines learn.

This concludes our section on why cognition on the cloud. In the next section, we are going to explore various Google Cloud AI services.

Google Cloud AI

Now that we understand what Cognition/AI on cloud ;is and why we need it, let's get started with learning the various Google Cloud AI services that are offered.

We have been briefly introduced to Google Cloud AI services in the GCP services section. Now let's dive deep into its offering.

In the next few subsections, we will be going through each of the services under the Google Cloud AI vertical.

Cloud AutoML ^{Alpha}

As of April 2018, Cloud AutoML is in alpha and is only available on request, subject to GCP terms and conditions.

AutoML helps us develop custom machine learning models with minimal ML knowledge and experience, using the power of Google's transfer learning and Neural Architecture Search technology.

Under this service, the first custom service that Google is releasing is named AutoML Vision This service will help users to train custom vision models for their own use cases.

There are other services that will follow.

Some of the key AutoML features are the following:

- Integration with human labeling
- Powered by Google's Transfer Learning and AutoML
- Fully integrated with other services of Google Cloud

You can read more about AutoML here: `https://cloud.google.com/automl/`.

Cloud TPU ^{Beta}

As of today, this service is in beta, but we need to explicitly request a TPU quota for our processing needs.

Using the Cloud TPUs, one can easily request large computation power to run our own machine learning algorithms. This service helps us with not only the required computing, but by using Google's TensorFlow, we can accelerate the complete setup.

This service can be used to perform heavy-duty machine learning, both training and prediction.

Some of the key Cloud TPU features are the following:

- High performance
- Utilizing the power of GCP
- Referencing data models
- Fully Integrated with other services of Google Cloud
- Connecting Cloud TPUs to custom machine types

You can read more about Cloud TPU here: `https://cloud.google.com/tpu/`.

Cloud Machine Learning Engine

Cloud Machine Learning Engine helps us easily build machine learning models that work on any type of data, of any size. Cloud Machine Learning Engine can take any TensorFlow model and perform large-scale training on a managed cluster. Additionally, it can also manage the trained models for large-scale online and batch predictions.

Cloud Machine Learning Engine can seamlessly transition from training to prediction, using online and batch prediction services. Cloud Machine Learning Engine uses the same scalable and distributed infrastructure with GPU acceleration that powers Google ML products.

Some of the key Cloud Machine Learning Engine features are the following:

- Fully integrated with other Google Cloud services
- Discover and Share Samples
- HyperTune your models
- Managed and Scalable Service
- Notebook Developer Experience
- Portable Models

You can read more about Cloud Machine Learning Engine here: `https://cloud.google.com/ml-engine/`.

Cloud Job Discovery Private ^{Beta}

Matching qualified people with the right people doesn't have to be so hard; that is the premise of **Cloud Job Discovery**.

Today's job portals and career sites search people for a job role based on keywords. This approach most of the time results in a mismatch of the candidate to the role. That is where Cloud Job Discovery comes into the picture to bridge the gap between employer and employee. **Job Discovery** provides plug-and-play access to Google's search and machine learning capabilities, enabling the entire recruiting ecosystem—company career sites, job boards, applicant-tracking systems, and staffing agencies—to improve job site engagement and candidate conversion.

Before we continue, you can navigate to `https://cloud.google.com/job-discovery/` and try out the **Job Discovery Demo**. You should see results based on your selection, similar to the following screenshot:

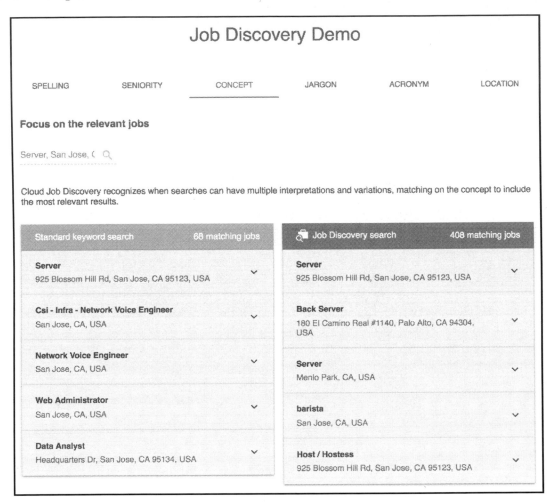

The key takeaway from the demo is how Discovery relates a profile to a keyword.

This diagram explains how Cloud Job Discovery works:

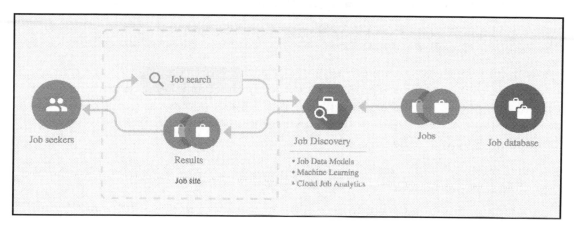

Some of the key differences of Cloud Job Discovery over a standard keyword search are the following:

- Keyword matching
- Company jargon recognition
- Abbreviation recognition
- Commute search
- Spelling correction
- Concept recognition
- Title detection
- Real-time query broadening
- Employer recognition
- Job enrichment
- Advanced location mapping
- Location expansion
- Seniority alignment

Dialogflow Enterprise Edition ^{Beta}

Dialogflow is a development suite which is used for building interfaces for websites, mobile applications, some of the popular machine learning platforms, and IoT devices.

It is powered by machine learning to recognize the intent and context of what a user says, allowing your conversational interface to provide highly efficient and accurate responses. Natural language understanding recognizes a user's intent and extracts prebuilt entities such as time, date, and numbers. You can train your agent to identify custom entity types by providing a small dataset of examples.

This service offers cross-platform and multi-language support and can work well with the Google Cloud speech service.

You can read more about Dialogflow Enterprise Edition here: `https://cloud.google.com/dialogflow-enterprise/`.

Cloud Natural Language

Google's **Cloud Natural Language** service helps us better understand the structure and meaning of a piece of text by providing powerful machine learning models.

These models can be queried by **REpresentational State Transfer (REST)** API. We can use it to understand sentiment about our product on social media, or parse intent from customer conversations happening in a call center or through a messaging app.

Before we continue with Cloud Natural Language, I would recommend heading over to `https://cloud.google.com/natural-language/` and trying out the API. Here is a quick glimpse of it:

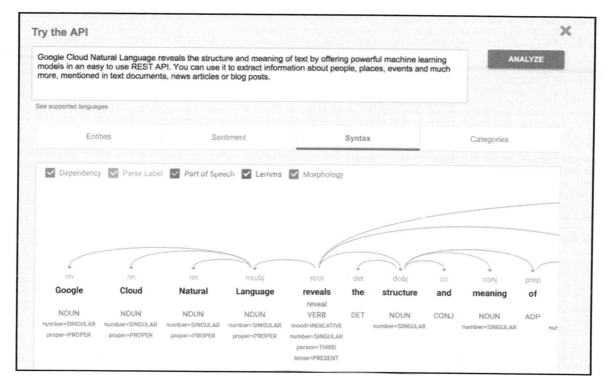

As we can see from the previous screenshot, this service offers various insights regarding a piece of text.

Some of the key features are:

- Syntax analysis
- Entity recognition
- Sentiment analysis
- Content classification
- Multi-language
- Integrated REST API

You can read more about Cloud Natural Language service here: `https://cloud.google.com/natural-language/`.

Cloud Speech API

Cloud Speech API uses powerful neural network models to convert audio to text in real time. This service is exposed as a REST API, as we have seen with the Google Cloud Natural Language API.

This API can recognize over 110 languages and users can use this service to convert speech to text in real time, recognize audio uploaded in the request, and integrate with our audio storage on Google Cloud Storage, by using the same technology Google uses to power its own products.

Before we continue with Cloud Speech API, I would recommend heading over to `https://cloud.google.com/speech/` and trying out the API. Here is a quick glimpse of it:

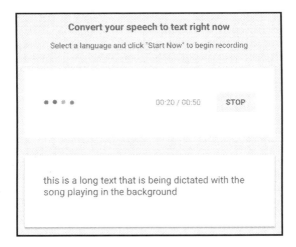

I was actually playing a song in the background and tried the speech-to-text. I was very impressed with the results, except for one part, where I said **with a song playing** and the API represented it as **with the song playing**; still, pretty good!

I think it is only a matter of time and continued use of these services that will increase their accuracy.

Some of the key features of Cloud Speech API are:

- **Automatic Speech Recognition (ASR)**
- Global vocabulary
- Streaming recognition

- Word hints
- Real-time or prerecorded audio support
- Noise robustness
- Inappropriate content filtering
- Integrated API

You can read more about Cloud Speech API here: `https://cloud.google.com/speech/`.

Cloud Translation API

Using the state-of-the-art **Neural Machine Translation**, the **Cloud Translation service** converts texts from one language to another.

Translation API is highly responsive, so websites and applications can integrate with Translation API for fast, dynamic translation of source text from the source language to a target language.

Before we continue with Cloud Translation API, I would recommend heading over to `https://cloud.google.com/translate/` and trying out the API. Here is a quick glimpse of it, as shown in the following screenshot:

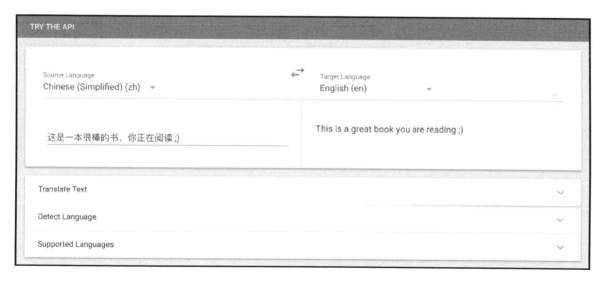

Some of the key features of Cloud Translation API are as follows:

- Programmatic access – REST API-driven
- Text translation
- Language detection
- Continuous updates

You can read more about Cloud Translate API here: `https://cloud.google.com/translate/`.

Cloud Vision API

Fred R. Barnard of Printers' Ink stated *"A picture is worth ten thousand words"*.

But no one really knows what those words are. Here comes the Google Cloud Vision API to decipher that for us.

Cloud Vision API takes an image as input and spits out the contents of the image as text. It can understand the contents of the image. And this service can be accessed over REST API.

Before we continue with Cloud Vision API, I would recommend heading over to `https://cloud.google.com/vision/` and trying out the API. Here is a quick glimpse of it as shown in the screenshot:

That is a photo of me when I was going through a *trying-to-grow-long-hair* phase, and after having fun at the beach. What is important is how the vision service was able to look at the image and detect my mood.

The same service can perform label detection as well as detect web entities related to this image among others.

Some of the key features of this service are:

- Detecting explicit content
- Detecting logos, labels, landmarks
- Landmark detection
- Optical character recognition
- Face detection
- Image attributes
- Integrated REST API

To find out more about Cloud Vision API, check this out: `https://cloud.google.com/vision/`.

Cloud Video Intelligence

Cloud Video Intelligence is one of the latest cognitive services released by Google. **Cloud Video Intelligence API** does almost all the things that the Cloud Vision API can do, but on videos.

This service extracts the metadata from a video frame by frame, and we can search any moment of the video file.

Before we continue with Cloud Video Intelligence, I would recommend heading over to `https://cloud.google.com/video-intelligence/` and trying out the API. Here is a quick glimpse of it, as shown in the screenshot:

I have selected the **dinosaur** and the **bicycle** video, and you can see the analysis.

Some of the key features of Cloud Video Intelligence are:

- Label detection
- Shot change detection
- Explicit content detection
- Video transcription [Alpha]

This concludes the overview of the various services offered as part of the Cloud AI vertical.

In this book, we are going to use a few of these to make a simple web application smart.

Summary

In this introductory chapter, we went through what Google Cloud Platform is and what services it offers. Next, we saw what Cloud Intelligence is and why we need it. After that, we went through the various services provide under the Cloud AI vertical.

In the next chapter, we are going to get started with exploring various Cloud AI services and how we can integrate them with the forum application, *SmartExchange*, which we are going to build.

Setting Up a Smart Forum App

2

In the last chapter, we saw what Google Cloud Platform is and what services it offers. We delved deep into one of its verticals, named Google Cloud AI, and went through all the services in that vertical. In this chapter, we are going to get started with our learning on Google Cloud AI services.. We are going to set up the base project in this chapter and build on top of it from the next chapter onward.

The topics to be covered in this chapter are:

- Design and architecture of *SmartExchange*
- Technology overview
- Project set up and exploration
- Deploying the base application to Heroku

Technical requirements

You will be required to have Node.js 6.13.1 installed on a system. Finally, to use the Git repository of this book, the user needs to install Git.

The code files of this chapter can be found on GitHub:
https://github.com/PacktPublishing/Google-Cloud-AI-Services-Quick-Start-Guide.

Check out the following video to see the code in action:
https://goo.gl/cViHRf.

SmartExchange architecture

The application we are going to build in this book is named *SmartExchange*. *SmartExchange* is a forum application, where registered users can create threads or topics of discussions and other users can like or reply to it. *SmartExchange* is not a full-fledged forum application but has all the key pieces needed to showcase the idea. As we keep moving toward the end of the book, we will be adding one Cloud AI service per chapter and will finally make the forum application a smart forum application. We are going to work with the following Cloud AI services:

- Cloud vision
- Video intelligence
- Speech recognition
- Cloud language processing
- Cloud translation

SmartExchange demo

Before getting started, you can take a look at the *SmartExchange* demo here: `https://smart-exchange.herokuapp.com`. This is the final application after we have added all the AI services to our application. The following screenshot shows the **Create New Thread** screen of the base application:

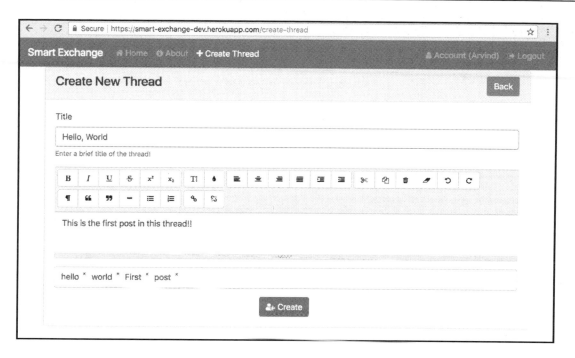

The following is the **Home** screen with a list of threads created by all users:

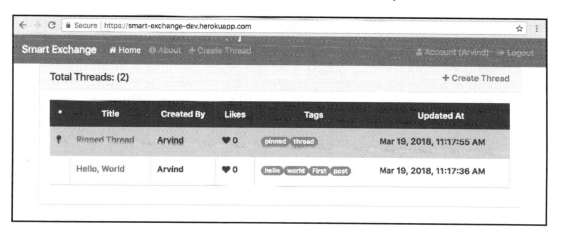

Architecture overview

Now that we have an idea as to what we are going to build, let's look at the architecture of this application. The following is the high-level design of the application:

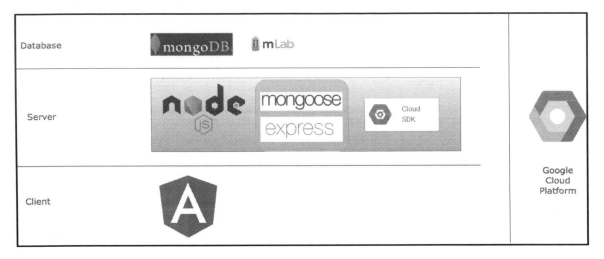

We are going to use MongoDB as our database, Node.js as our server-side layer and Angular 5 as our application layer. We are going to use a Node.js Google Cloud SDK module to interface our application with the Google Cloud Platform. For the MongoDB instance, we are going to use the mLab (`https://mlab.com/`) service and connect that to our application. We are going to set up mLab as part of this chapter.

On the server side, we are using Node.js (`https://nodejs.org`) as the runtime environment. We are going to use Express (`https://expressjs.com`) as our server side MVC framework. Using Mongoose, we are going to interface with MongoDB.

On the client side, we are going to Angular [5.x] (`https://angular.io/`) as our application layer. Since we would be working with various Cloud AI services from Google Cloud Platform, we are going to use Google Cloud SDK npm module depending on the service we are interfacing with. Once we build the application, we are going to deploy it to Heroku (`https://www.heroku.com/`).

Database design

In this section, we are going to look at the database design. We are going to have three collections; namely, user, thread and message. Any visitor to our forum will be able to view the threads and replies. But they cannot post a reply or create a thread or like a reply/thread till they log in. The user collection will have the following schema:

- **Name**: User's full name.
- **Email**: User's email address.
- **Password**: User's login password.
- **Role**: Will have two values, user and admin. The default value is user.

The thread collection will have the following schema:

- **Title**: The title of the thread.
- **Description**: The description of the thread.
- **Tags**: The searchable tags for the thread.
- **Is Pinned**: The boolean values that pins this thread on top of other threads. Default is false.
- **Likes**: The number of likes on this thread. Default zero.
- **Created By**: The MongoDB Object ID of the user who has created this thread.
- **Created At**: The time at which the record was created.
- **Last Update By**: The MongoDB Object ID of the user who has updated this thread.
- **Last Update At**: The time at which the record was updated.

The message collection will have the following schema:

- **Thread**: The MongoDB Object ID of the thread to which this message belongs to.
- **Description**: The message contents.
- **Likes**: The number of likes on this thread. Default zero.
- **Created By**: The MongoDB Object ID of the user who has created this message.
- **Created At**: The time at which the record was created
- **Last Update By**: The MongoDB Object ID of the user who has updated this message.
- **Last Update At**: The time at which the record was updated.

We will be updating the message schema as we keep working with various Google Cloud AI services. This concludes the database schema walk-through. In the next section, we are going to look at the APIs exposed by *SmartExchange* app.

APIs

SmartExchange exposes the following API end points to the outside world:

Name	Description	Authorization	Route
Register user	Registers new user taking in email, password and name as inputs	No	`/api/register`
Login user	Logins in user taking in email and password as inputs	No	`/api/login`
Get threads	Gets a list of threads in the database	No	`/api/threads`
Create thread	Creates a new thread by taking title, description and tags as inputs	Yes	`/api/thread`
Edit thread	Updates an existing thread	Yes	`/api/thread/threadId`
Delete thread	Deletes an existing thread	Yes	`/api/thread/threadId`
Create message	Creates a new message on a thread by passing in the message as input	Yes	`/api/message`
Edit message	Updates an existing message	Yes	`/api/message/messageId`
Delete message	Deletes an existing message	Yes	`/api/message/messageId`

Setting up the project

Now that we are aware of the high-level architecture, let's get started by setting up the environment to develop the project. To develop and run the application locally, we need to have the following dependencies installed:

1. Git
2. Node.js
3. MongoDB (optional)
4. Angular CLI
5. Yarn (optional)
6. Heroku Toolbelt (optional)

Installing Git

To install Git, head over to `https://git-scm.com/book/en/v2/Getting-Started-Installing-Git` and follow the instructions on that page to install Git for your OS. Once you have successfully installed, you can run the following command to verify the installation:

```
$ git --version
git version 2.11.0 (Apple Git-81)
```

Installing Node.js

To install Node.js, head over to `https://nodejs.org/download/release/v6.13.1/` and download the appropriate installer for your OS. The application we are going to build is going to be running on node 6.13.x and npm 3.10.x. Once you have successfully installed, you can run the following command to verify the installation:

```
$ node -v
v6.13.1
$ npm -v
3.10.10
```

Installing MongoDB (optional)

For this application, we are going to use mLab (https://mlab.com/) to host our database as a service. But if you would like to install MongoDB for your local development, you can do so from here: https://docs.mongodb.com/manual/installation/. Once MongoDB is successfully installed, you can run the following command to verify the installation:

```
$ mongo --version
MongoDB shell version v3.4.10
git version: 078f28920cb24de0dd479b5ea6c66c644f6326e9
OpenSSL version: OpenSSL 1.0.2m 2 Nov 2017
allocator: system
modules: none
build environment:
    distarch: x86_64
    target_arch: x86_64
```

We are going to use MongoDB 3.4 for our application.

Angular CLI

Now that Node.js has been installed, let's install Angular CLI (https://cli.angular.io). Open a Command Prompt / Terminal and run the following command:

```
$ npm install -g @angular/cli@1.7.3
```

Once you have successfully installed, you can run the following command to verify the installation:

```
$ ng -v
```

```
    _                      _                 ____ _     ___
   / \   _ __   __ _ _   _| | __ _ _ __     / ___| |   |_ _|
  / △ \ | '_ \ / _` | | | | |/ _` | '__|   | |   | |    | |
 / ___ \| | | | (_| | |_| | | (_| | |      | |___| |___ | |
/_/   \_\_| |_|\__, |\__,_|_|\__,_|_|       \____|_____|___|
               |___/

Angular CLI: 1.7.3
Node: 6.13.1
OS: darwin x64
Angular:
...
```

Yarn (optional)

Yarn (https://yarnpkg.com/en) is another package manager similar to npm. Yarn has its own share of advantages of npm (https://www.sitepoint.com/yarn-vs-npm/). If you are comfortable with Yarn over npm, you can use that too. You can install Yarn using npm as shown in the following command:

```
$ npm install -g yarn
```

Once Yarn has been successfully installed, we can verify the same by running the following:

```
$ yarn -v
1.5.1
```

We are using Yarn version 1.5.1 for working with our application.

Heroku Toolbelt (optional)

If you would like to deploy this application to Heroku, you need to create a new Heroku account https://signup.heroku.com/, if you do not already have one. And you need to install the Heroku Toolbelt. Navigate to: https://devcenter.heroku.com/articles/heroku-cli#download-and-install to download and install.

Text editors (optional)

You can use any text editor of your choice. I use Sublime Text 3 (https://www.sublimetext.com/3) with the following packages installed:

- Emmet
- HTML-CSS-JS-Prettify
- SCSS
- TypeScript
- TypeScript completion

Alternatively, you can use Visual Studio Code (https://code.visualstudio.com/) or Atom (https://atom.io/) or any other editor of your choice.

Setting up mLab

Now that we have set up all our local dependencies, we are going to set up mLab account. If you already have a mLab account, you can skip this section. The following are the steps to set up your mLab account:

1. To create an mLab account, navigate to `https://mlab.com/signup/` and create a new account. Verify your email and log into your account.

2. Now that we have logged in, we will create a new database. From the **Home** page of mLab, click on **Create New** button. For our application, we are going to use a free plan database.

3. On the **Cloud Provider** page, select as shown in the following screenshot:

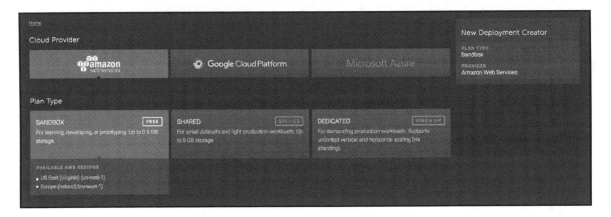

4. Click on **Continue** to proceed.
5. Now select a region based on your location. I have selected **Europe**.
6. Click **Continue** to proceed.

7. In the following screen, provide a database name. I have provided `smart-exchange`.

8. Click **Continue** and verify your order:

9. Finally, click on **Submit Order**. This will take a moment and create a new database for us.

10. Once the database is created, click on the database name from the **Home** page and you should land on a screen similar to in the following screenshot:

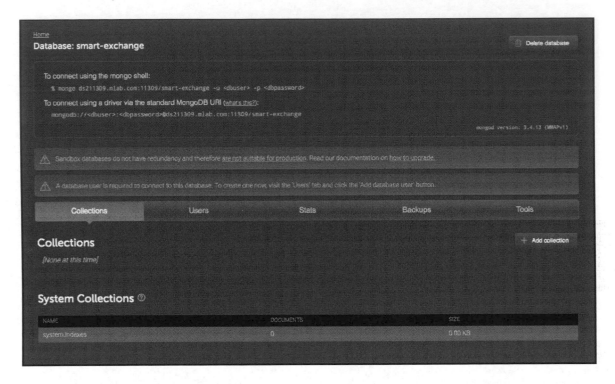

You will see a couple of warnings. The first one states that this database is not suitable for production and we are aware of it. The second one indicates that we do not have a database admin user. Let's create that one in the next section.

11. For creating database admin, click on the **Users** tab and then click on **Add new database user** and a popup should ope, as shown in the following screenshot:

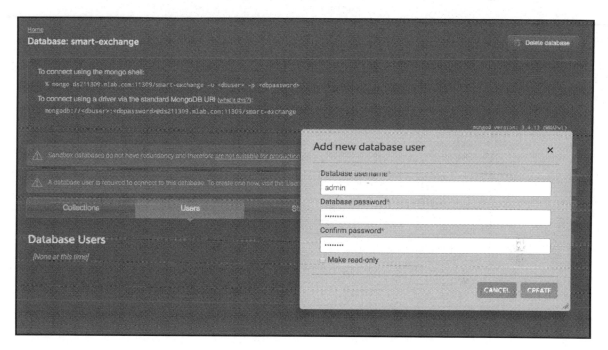

I have provided the username as `admin` and password as `admin123` for convenience. You can update it as applicable. Then, click on **CREATE** and we should see a new database user created and the second warning also vanishes.

Test connection

Now that we have set up our database and the database user, let's test the connection. On the mLab database page, you should see the section shown in the following screenshot:

This is our connection string, using which we can connect to the database from our application or from mongo shell or from a GUI tool like Robo 3T. If you have MongoDB installed locally, you can test the connection from the mongo shell using the command as shown. Open a new Terminal/Prompt and run:

```
$ mongo ds211309.mlab.com:11309/smart-exchange -u admin -p admin123
```

We should see that the connection succeeded as shown in the following screenshot:

```
↪  ~ mongo ds211309.mlab.com:11309/smart-exchange -u admin -p admin123
MongoDB shell version v3.4.10
connecting to: mongodb://ds211309.mlab.com:11309/smart-exchange
MongoDB server version: 3.4.13
rs-ds211309:PRIMARY> db.stats()
{
        "db" : "smart-exchange",
        "collections" : 2,
        "views" : 0,
        "objects" : 1,
        "avgObjSize" : 48,
        "dataSize" : 48,
        "storageSize" : 12288,
        "numExtents" : 2,
        "indexes" : 0,
        "indexSize" : 0,
        "fileSize" : 16777216,
        "nsSizeMB" : 1,
        "extentFreeList" : {
                "num" : 8,
                "totalSize" : 1597440
        },
        "dataFileVersion" : {
                "major" : 4,
                "minor" : 22
        },
        "ok" : 1
}
rs-ds211309:PRIMARY> ▊
```

This concludes our connection test.

Update the connection string above with your connection string; otherwise, you will be connecting to my database.

Robo 3T connection (optional)

It is always good to have a database client command-line or otherwise to quickly debug what is going on from the database end. I have used a few GUI tools for MongoDB and found Robo 3T previously known as Robomongo to be a good choice. You can navigate to `https://robomongo.org/download` and download Robo 3T for your OS.

The following are the steps for Robo 3T connection:

1. Once installed and launched, you can click on **File | Connect**. In the following popup click on **Create** and update the **Connection** tab as shown in the following screenshot:

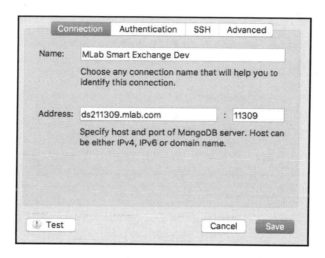

2. Update the **Authentication** tab as shown in the following screenshot:

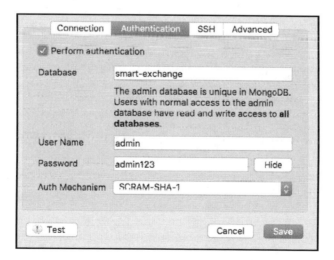

3. Leave the **SSH** tab as is. Finally, update the **Advanced** tab as shown in the following screenshot:

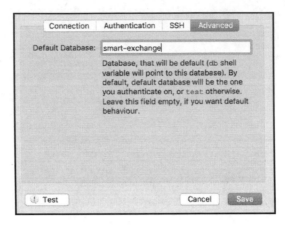

4. Click on **Test** to test the connection and **Save** the connection
5. Once you have saved the connection, click on the new connection entity we have created and click **Connect** and we should be logged into the database from the GUI and be able execute queries as shown in the following screenshot:

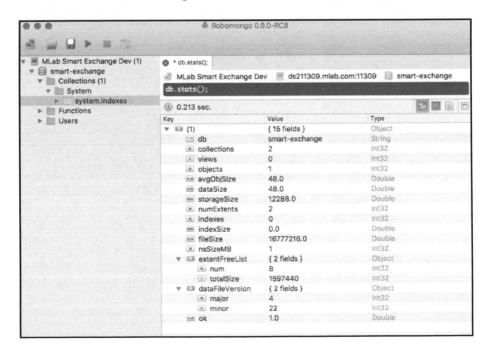

This concludes our walk-through of required dependencies. In the next section, we will get started with the code set up.

Setting up an authentication

When working with any Google Cloud AI service, we need to have either an API key or a service account key set up. In this section, we are going to set up both, so you can use any approach to explore. Before we set up the API key or a service account, we need to have a Google Cloud project. If you already have a project, you can skip this section.

Creating the project

To create a new project, follow the below steps:

1. Navigate to Google Platform Console: `https://console.cloud.google.com/`
2. Create a new project using the project selector menu form the top navigation bar of the page
3. I have created a new project for this book named as `SmartExchange` and have given a custom project ID as `smart-exchange-b10882`, you can pick which ever you are comfortable with

This is the project we are going to use for this book and we are going to enable all the required keys and APIs on this project.

Setting up API key

Now that we have a project, let's set up an API key first. Follow these steps:

1. Navigate to Google Platform Console: `https://console.cloud.google.com/`
2. Select the project we have created
3. From the menu on the left-hand side, select **APIs & Services**
4. Once you are on **APIs & Services** page, from the menu on the left-hand side, select **Credentials**

5. Using the **Create Credentials** drop down on the page, select **API key**

6. This will generate an API key, copy that key and protect it as you would a secure password

We will be using this key soon to explore the Vision API

Setting up service account key

Now that we have a project and an API key, let's set up a Service Account Key as well. Follow these steps:

1. Navigate to Google Platform Console: https://console.cloud.google.com/
2. Select the project we have created
3. From the menu on the left-hand side, select **APIs & Services**
4. Once you are on **APIs & Services** page, from the menu on the left-hand side, select **Credentials**
5. Using the **Create Credentials** dropdown on the page, select **Service account key**
6. Under **Service account** dropdown, select **New service account** and fill it as below
    1. **Service account name**: smart-exchange-service-account
    2. **Role**: **Project| Owner** (do not use this role in production, provide access to only the required services)
7. Leave the auto generated **Service account ID** as is
8. Under **key type**, select **JSON**
9. Click on **Create** and you should be prompted to download a JSON file.
10. Download and save this file securely and protect it as you would a secure password.

We will be using a service account key when we make a service call from our application using the SDK. The SDK expects this JSON file's path to be exposed using a environment variable named GOOGLE_APPLICATION_CREDENTIALS and the value as the path to the JSON file. If you are using an *nix-based OS, you can set this value from the Command Prompt as follows:

```
export GOOGLE_APPLICATION_CREDENTIALS=/Users/arvindravulavaru/Downloads/
SmartExchange-29e9aed0a8aa.json
```

Or you can add the same to `bashrc` or `profile` or `zshrc` file.

On Windows, you can use:

```
setx GOOGLE_APPLICATION_CREDENTIALS "C:/Users/arvindravulavaru/Downloads/
SmartExchange-29e9aed0a8aa.json"
```

For more help on setting environment variables, refer: `https://www.schrodinger.com/kb/1842`. We will be using this later on when we are integrating the API with our application.

Setting up code

Now that we have all the tools needed to start developing the application, we will go through the list of technology pre-requisites:

- *SmartExchange* application is completely written in TypeScript (`https://www.typescriptlang.org`). TypeScript is a typed superset of JavaScript that compiles to plain JavaScript. If you are new to TypeScript, here is a video series on getting started with TypeScript: `https://www.youtube.com/watch?v=hADI92zCIvE&list=PLYxzS__5yYQkX-95LHG5EDxPj3tVvVmRd`.

- On the server side, we are going to use Mongoose to interface with the MongoDB. Mongoose is a MongoDB object-modelling tool designed to work with asynchronous environment. If you are new to Mongoose, here is a video series on getting started with Mongoose: `https://www.youtube.com/watch?v=swWRUvluSkE&list=PLGquJ_T_JBMQ1C0Pp41sykceli8G1UGtg`.

- Express is going to be our service side MVC framework. If you are new to Express, here is a video series on Express from scratch: `https://www.youtube.com/watch?v=k_0ZzvHbNBQ&list=PLillGF-RfqbYRpji8t4SxUkMxfowG4Kqp`.

- Finally, on the client side, we are going to use Angular framework, Version 5.2.0. If you are aware of Angular 2.x or above, most of the code should be familiar. If you are new to Angular 5 altogether, you can checkout this video series: `https://www.youtube.com/watch?v=0cWrpsCLMJQ&list=PLC3y8-rFHvwhBRAgFinJR8KHIrCdTkZcZ`.

To get the combined knowledge of an entire *MEAN stack* application, take a look at the video entitled Setting up a MEAN4+ App (MongoDB, Express.js, Nodejs, Angular): `https://www.youtube.com/watch?v=Tw-rskOmcMM`. Make sure you have at least a basic understanding of the above before you continue.

Downloading base code

Let's get started with the actual code now. On your machine where you have installed all your dependencies, create a new folder named `SmartExchange`. Open Command Prompt or Terminal inside that folder. Navigate to `https://github.com/PacktPublishing/getting-started-with-google-cloud-ai-services` and you should find a folder in this repository named `Chapter 2\code\smart-exchange-base`.

If you would like, you can download the entire repository that consists of completed code chapter by chapter, or you can explicitly download the code of one folder using a service such as GitZip. To use GitZip, head over to `http://kinolien.github.io/gitzip/` and paste `https://github.com/PacktPublishing/Getting-Started-with-Google-Cloud-AI-Services/tree/master/Chapter%202/code/smart-exchange-base%20` in the text box at the top right-hand corner. This will download only the `smart-exchange-base` folder.

Once you have successfully downloaded the `smart-exchange-base` folder, `cd` into the`smart-exchange-base` folder from your Command Prompt / Terminal. We have a `package.json` file at the root of the `smart-exchange-base` folder. This file has all the required dependencies listed. We would need to install them to get started. Run the following command:

```
$ npm install
or
$ yarn install
```

This will install all the dependencies listed. Next, open the entire application in your favorite editor, and then open `README.md`. This file gives you a quick overview of this app.

As it states here, the base template is created by Davide Violante (`https://github.com/DavideViolante`) and I have customized it for this book. The original repoistory can be found here: `https://github.com/DavideViolante/Angular-Full-Stack`. This is one of the latest repositories I have found that has all the key ingredients for developing a production grade application. I have added a bunch of things on top of it to make it a bit more robust.

Once the installation is completed, let's actually set up the Database connection URL. Open `.env` file present at the root of the folder and update the `MONGODB_URI` value to the connection string that you have created, the one from mLab. We will walk-through the code in a few moments, which will explain where which value is used. If you leave the connection string as is, you will see an error, as my database no longer exists.

Once you have updated the connection, head back to Command Prompt / Terminal and run the following:

```
$ npm run dev
or
$ yarn dev
```

This will concurrently start the Angular CLI server with a proxy to `3000` port on the same machine, which is where our Express server is running, run the TypeScript compiler on the `server` folder, and execute the `app.js` present in the `dist/server` folder on port `3000`.

Once the command has finished executing, it will launch the application on your default browser at `http://localhost:4200/` and will serve the home page. If everything goes well, we should see something such as this:

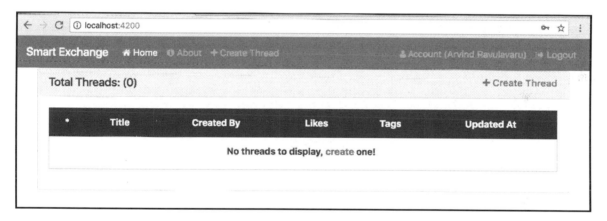

Note, if you would like to use a local instance of MongoDB instead of mLab, you can update MongoDB URI as follows:

```
MONGODB_URI=mongodb://localhost:27017/smart-exchange
```

Use the following command:

```
$ npm run dev:local
or
$ yarn dev:local
```

This script will start the local MongoDB instance as well, along with other initializations. Now that we have set up the project and run it to see the output, lets walk through the code.

App folder structure

The app folder structure would be as follows:

```
.
├── .env
├── CREDITS
├── LICENSE
├── Procfile
├── README.md
├── client
│   ├── app
│   ├── assets
│   ├── environments
│   ├── index.html
│   ├── main.ts
│   ├── polyfills.ts
│   ├── styles.css
│   ├── test.ts
│   ├── tsconfig.app.json
│   ├── tsconfig.spec.json
│   └── typings.d.ts
├── dist
│   ├── 3rdpartylicenses.txt
│   ├── assets
│   ├── fontawesome-webfont.674f50d287a8c48dc19b.eot
│   ├── fontawesome-webfont.912ec66d7572ff821749.svg
│   ├── fontawesome-webfont.af7ae505a9eed503f8b8.woff2
│   ├── fontawesome-webfont.b06871f281fee6b241d6.ttf
│   ├── fontawesome-webfont.fee66e712a8a08eef580.woff
│   ├── index.html
│   ├── inline.318b50c57b4eba3d437b.bundle.js
│   ├── main.3c287c0a94f89fea8f5d.bundle.js
│   ├── polyfills.7f7a52ac900057ac4964.bundle.js
│   ├── scripts.387e44acce16cb817b45.bundle.js
│   ├── server
│   └── styles.1cd1653d033af7313cc4.bundle.css
├── e2e
│   ├── app.e2e-spec.ts
│   ├── app.po.ts
│   └── tsconfig.e2e.json
├── karma.conf.js
├── package.json
├── protractor.conf.js
├── proxy.conf.json
├── server
│   ├── app.ts
```

```
|   ├──── auth
|   ├──── controllers
|   ├──── models
|   ├──── routes
|   ├──── routes.ts
|   ├──── test
|   └──── tsconfig.json
├──── tsconfig.json
└──── tslint.json
```

Here is a quick overview of its contents:

- `.env`: This file defines all the environment variables for our application.
- `CREDITS`: This consists of the credits to the assets which we have used.
- `LICENSE`: This project is MIT licensed by Davide Violante and Arvind Ravulavaru.
- `Procfile`: The contents of this file will be used when working with Heroku deployment.
- `README.md`: This onsists of basic information about the project, and how to use and deploy the code.
- `client`: This folder consists of our Angular code. Any client side application development would be done here.
- `dist`: This folder is our final output folder, which can be deployed on to any server running Node.js.
- `e2e`: This folder consists of Angular end-to-end testing test cases. I have not modified these or added any as part of this application.
- `karma.conf.js`: This consists of Karma configuration. Karma is a test runner.
- `package.json`: This file consists of the dependencies of the project as well as the scripts that we are going to use to run and deploy our application.
- `protractor.conf.js`: This file consists of the Angular end-to- end testing framework named Protractor.
- `proxy.conf.json`: This is a development file that proxies the Express server running on port 3000 to `/api` endpoint. This would not be done during production.
- `server`: This folder consists of our *Express Mongoose* application. All server side development will happen here.
- `tsconfig.json`: This file consists of the TypeScript configuration for this project.

Above is a quick `app` folder structure walk-through. In the next section, we are going to walk-through the server code.

Server code walk-through

Everything on the server starts from the `server\app.ts` file. In this file, we have imported the required dependencies for our *Express* application. We have also imported set routes which define all the APIs that we are exposing from this application.

Express and Mongoose

To initialize the database connection, we are pulling in the `MONGODB_URI` that we have defined inside the `.env` file. We are feeding this to `mongoose.connect()` to initialize the database connection. Once MongoDB has been connected, we execute `setRoutes()` to initialize the routes and dispatch a static message if any reaches `http://localhost:3000/` directly during development.

Routes

The next thing we are going to look at is the routes. Open `server\routes.ts` file and we should see three imports, which define the three API services that we have. `defineUserRoutes` imports all the routes for User API, `defineThreadRoutes` imports all the routes for Thread API, and `defineMessageRoutes` imports all the routes for Message API. Navigate to `server\routes\user.ts`, `server\routes\thread.ts` and `server\routes\message.ts` to view the routes listed.

Security

The application we have built uses JSON Web Token (`https://jwt.io/`) based authentication. Navigate to `server\auth\index.ts` and `createJWToken`, `Authenticate` and `Authorize` methods exported. `createJWToken` is used to create a new JWT token, taking in the user object as input.

The expiry time of the token is defined by TOKEN_MAXAGE that is defined in the .env file. Authenticate is an Express middleware, that processes the incoming request looking for the JWT token. Then this token is decoded and the user is fetched. Authorize is also an express middleware that authorizes whether a specific role user can access a specific type of API. For example, if we head over to server\routes\user.ts and look at router.delete('/user/:id', Authenticate, Authorize('admin'), userCtrl.delete);, we can clearly see that a user who is trying to access the user delete API should be authenticated with a valid JWT and then authorized by being an admin. This way we protect our assets on the server side, even if client side validation fails.

Mongoose models

Next, we are going to look at the Mongoose models. As we have seen earlier, we have three collections in the database and we have three Mongoose models associated with these collections. You can find the models inside the server\models folder. The server\models\user.ts has the models and password encryption and validation logic present. server\models\thread.ts has the model to work with thread collection, and server\models\message.ts has the model to work with message collection.

Controllers

Now that we have the models and routes, let's look at the controllers that process the API request. All the controllers are placed inside server\controllers folder. All the controllers that we have created so far extend (https://www.typescriptlang.org/docs/handbook/classes.html) from the BaseCtrl. BaseCtrl implements all the basic CRUD operations for a model. These operations include:

- getAll. Get all documents in a collection
- count: Count of all documents in that collection
- insert: Create a new document in that collection
- get: Get a document by its _id
- update: Update a document
- delete: Delete a document by its _id

If we look at `server\controllers\user.ts`, it extends `BaseCtrl` and then defines, the model as `User`. Apart from that, we have created a method of our own named `login` that can authenticate a user and respond accordingly. If the login is successful, we will send the user object along with a JWT; otherwise, we send back a `403 forbidden` message. This concludes our walk-through of the server side code. Now lets look at the client side code.

Client code walk-through

The client in our application is Angular 5.2.0 and it resides inside the `client` folder. The documentation for this folder can be found here: `https://smart-exchange.herokuapp. com/docs/`. Everything starts from the `client\index.html` file. This file consists of our `approot`. `client\app\app.module.ts` defines all the `declaration`, `imports`, `providers`, `schemas`, and the `bootstrap` component.

Our `app-root` component is defined here: `client\app\app.component.ts` and the corresponding HTML is defined here: `client\app\app.component.html`. This file defines our navigation bar and places a `router-outlet` where all the remaining routes of the application get inserted.

Routing

All the client side routes are defined in `client\app\routing.module.ts`. Our default page is `HomeComponent`. Apart from home, we have the following routes: `about`, `create-thread`, `view-thread`, `edit-thread`, `register`, `login`, `logout`, `account`, `admin`, and `notfound`. If the route we are navigating to is not listed above, we redirect the user to `notfound` route. As we can see from this file, all routes mention the component that gets invoked when this route is active.

Apart from that, we have a `canActivate` attribute, which defines an `AuthGuardLogin` or `AuthGuardAdmin` service. This service is responsible for not letting in the *not logged in* users access that route.

Authentication

We have two service named `AuthGuardAdmin` and `AuthGuardLogin`.

- `AuthGuardAdmin`: Checks whether the current logged in user is an admin. If they are, they are allowed to navigate. The path for this service is `client\app\services\auth-guard-admin.service.ts`.
- `AuthGuardLogin`: Checks whether a user is logged in. If they are, they are allowed to navigate. The path for this service is `client\app\services\auth-guard-login.service.ts`.

Services

Apart from the two services we have just mentioned, we have five more services:

- `AuthService`:
  The path for this service is: `client\app\services\auth.service.ts`.
  This service defines four methods:
  `getCurrentUser`, `login`, `logout`, and `setCurrentUser`.
- `UserService`:
  The path for this service is `client\app\services\user.service.ts`.
  This service defines seven methods: `register`, `login`, `getUsers`, `countUsers`, `getUser`, `editUser`, and `deleteUser`.
- `ThreadService`:
  The path for this service is `client\app\services\thread.service.ts`.
  This service defines six methods: `getThreads`, `countThreads`, `addThread`, `getThread`, `editThread`, and `deleteThread`.
- `MessageService`:
  The path for this service is `client\app\services\message.service.ts`.
  This service defines three methods: `addMessage`, `editMessage`, and `deleteMessage`.

These services are quite self-explanatory. Apart from these, there is another service named `TokenInterceptor`: `client\app\services\http.interceptor.ts`. This service implements `HttpInterceptor`. In this service, we intercept every incoming and outgoing request. For every outgoing request, we add an authorization header assigning the value of JWT token that we have saved in local storage, if the token is present. And for every incoming request, we check the response status code. If the status code is `401` or `403`, we kick the user out of the application and show message that they have performed an unauthorized activity.

Components

The final entity we are going to look at is the components. For this section, instead of pointing to the code in the text editor, I will refer to the hosted documentation. The hosted documentation has additional information that we are going to see in a moment. You can read more about these components, under the **Components** section, here: `https://smart-exchange.herokuapp.com/docs/`. Here is the list of key components on the client site:

- **Home**: This is the home component, which loads by default. This route loads the list of threads that are created by various users and sorts them by time, as well as pinned threads. Also, do take a look at the **DOM Tree** tab: `https://smart-exchange.herokuapp.com/docs/components/HomeComponent.html#dom-tree`. These will give you more insight into this component.
- **About**: This component displays a static page that talks about the application.
- **Register**: This component has the logic and mark up needed to register a new user.
- **Login**: This component has the logic and mark up needed to login a registered user.
- **Account**: This component has the logic and mark up needed to display user's profile. We are not providing an option as of now to edit the profile.
- **Admin**: This component has the logic and mark up to view a list of users in database. This component can be accessed only by an admin. By default, when a user registers using the application, they will be assigned a *user* role. If we want to change this, we need to log into the database manually and then update *user* to admin.
- **Create thread**: This component has the logic and mark up to create a new thread. Only logged in users have access to this component.
- **Edit thread**: This component has the logic and mark up to edit a created thread. Only the owner of the thread or an admin can access this component.

- **View thread**: This component has the logic and mark up to view a thread as well as the replies on that thread. In the same component, we have set up the form to reply to this thread. Only logged in users can reply.

These are some of the key components on the client site. This wraps up our walk-through of the client side code. In the next section, we will run the application and observe the output.

Running the app

Now that we have a good understanding of the code base, lets go back to the Command Prompt or Terminal and run the application, if it is not already running. You can use the following command to run the application:

```
$ npm run dev
or
$ yarn dev
```

This will launch the default browser and navigate you to `http://localhost:4200/`. Let's register with the application and, to do that, navigate to the register page using the menu link. Create a new account with your details.

If everything goes well, you should see a success message and be redirected to the login page. Log in with the newly created credentials, and if everything goes well, we will be logged into the application and we should see a screen as shown in the following screenshot:

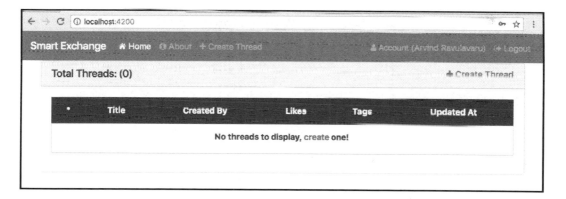

Before we go further, lets take a quick peek at the database. You can use either mongo shell or Robo 3T or mLab interface itself to view this data. I have used mongo shell and here is the user's collection:

```
→  smart-exchange-base  mongo ds211309.mlab.com:11309/smart-exchange -u admin -p admin123
MongoDB shell version v3.4.10
connecting to: mongodb://ds211309.mlab.com:11309/smart-exchange
MongoDB server version: 3.4.13
rs-ds211309:PRIMARY> show collections;
system.indexes
users
rs-ds211309:PRIMARY> db.users.find({}).pretty();
{
        "_id" : ObjectId("5aafb06ec790687418346c68"),
        "name" : "Arvind Ravulavaru",
        "email" : "arvind@myapp.com",
        "password" : "$2a$10$AA5PAReQYgfIlfHBkIYgX.w7HQlWNcgzGuRDQjUIzvMmtCul5l8xe",
        "role" : "user",
        "__v" : 0
}
rs-ds211309:PRIMARY> 
```

Next, let's create a thread. Click on **Create New Thread** button and fill the form as shown in the following screenshot:

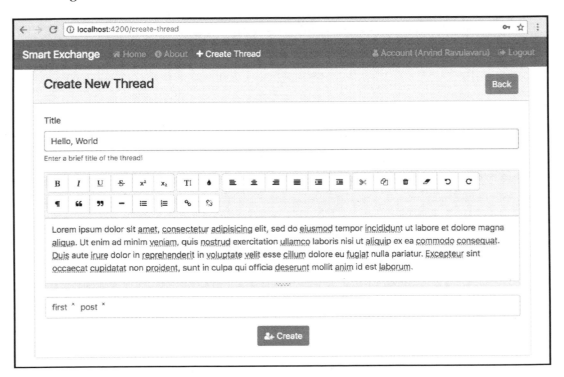

Click on **Create**. The database snapshot of the same would be as follows:

```
→ smart-exchange-base  mongo ds211309.mlab.com:11309/smart-exchange -u admin -p admin123
MongoDB shell version v3.4.10
connecting to: mongodb://ds211309.mlab.com:11309/smart-exchange
MongoDB server version: 3.4.13
rs-ds211309:PRIMARY> show collections;
system.indexes
threads
users
rs-ds211309:PRIMARY> db.threads.find({}).pretty();
{
        "_id" : ObjectId("5aafb1d2c790687418346c69"),
        "title" : "Hello, World",
        "description" : "Lorem ipsum dolor sit amet, consectetur adipisicing elit, sed do eiusmod tempor incididu
nt ut labore et dolore magna aliqua. Ut enim ad minim veniam, quis nostrud exercitation ullamco laboris nisi ut a
liquip ex ea commodo consequat. Duis aute irure dolor in reprehenderit in voluptate velit esse cillum dolore eu f
ugiat nulla pariatur. Excepteur sint occaecat cupidatat non proident, sunt in culpa qui officia deserunt mollit a
nim id est laborum.",
        "tags" : [
                {
                        "displayValue" : "first"
                },
                {
                        "displayValue" : "post"
                }
        ],
        "isPinned" : false,
        "createdBy" : ObjectId("5aafb06ec790687418346c68"),
        "lastUpdatedBy" : ObjectId("5aafb06ec790687418346c68"),
        "likes" : 0,
        "createdAt" : ISODate("2018-03-19T12:49:22.351Z"),
        "lastUpdateAt" : ISODate("2018-03-19T12:49:22.351Z"),
        "__v" : 0
}
rs-ds211309:PRIMARY> 
```

Click on the thread title on the home page and it will take you to the view thread page. Click on the *heart* to add a like to this thread. You can click as many times as you want and the likes increase. This is the way I have designed it—unconditional love. You are free to redesign the application as you please. To pin the thread, you can click on edit thread icon and check the **Pin this thread** checkbox and **Save**.

Your thread list on the home page should look like this:

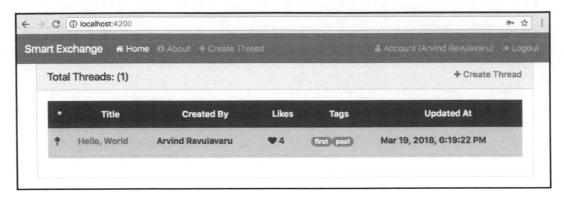

The database snapshot would be as follows:

```
→ smart-exchange-base  mongo ds211309.mlab.com:11309/smart-exchange -u admin -p admin123
MongoDB shell version v3.4.10
connecting to: mongodb://ds211309.mlab.com:11309/smart-exchange
MongoDB server version: 3.4.13
rs-ds211309:PRIMARY> show collections;
system.indexes
threads
users
rs-ds211309:PRIMARY> db.threads.find({}).pretty();
{
        "_id" : ObjectId("5aafb1d2c790687418346c69"),
        "title" : "Hello, World",
        "description" : "Lorem ipsum dolor sit amet, consectetur adipisicing elit, sed do eiusmod tempor incididu
nt ut labore et dolore magna aliqua. Ut enim ad minim veniam, quis nostrud exercitation ullamco laboris nisi ut a
liquip ex ea commodo consequat. Duis aute irure dolor in reprehenderit in voluptate velit esse cillum dolore eu f
ugiat nulla pariatur. Excepteur sint occaecat cupidatat non proident, sunt in culpa qui officia deserunt mollit a
nim id est laborum.",
        "tags" : [
                {
                        "displayValue" : "first"
                },
                {
                        "displayValue" : "post"
                }
        ],
        "isPinned" : true,
        "createdBy" : ObjectId("5aafb06ec790687418346c68"),
        "lastUpdatedBy" : ObjectId("5aafb06ec790687418346c68"),
        "likes" : 4,
        "createdAt" : ISODate("2018-03-19T12:49:22.351Z"),
        "lastUpdateAt" : ISODate("2018-03-19T12:49:22.351Z"),
        "__v" : 0
}
rs-ds211309:PRIMARY>
```

Now, lets add reply to thread. Click on thread title and navigate to the view thread page. Under the comments section, fill the form with your reply and post it. This will add a new reply to the thread and a new document to the message collection as shown in the following screenshot:

```
→ smart-exchange-base  mongo ds211309.mlab.com:11309/smart-exchange -u admin -p admin123
MongoDB shell version v3.4.10
connecting to: mongodb://ds211309.mlab.com:11309/smart-exchange
MongoDB server version: 3.4.13
rs-ds211309:PRIMARY> show collections;
messages
system.indexes
threads
users
rs-ds211309:PRIMARY> db.messages.find({}).pretty();
{
        "_id" : ObjectId("5aafb438c790687418346c6a"),
        "thread" : ObjectId("5aafb1d2c790687418346c69"),
        "description" : "Neque porro quisquam est qui dolorem ipsum quia dolor sit amet, consectetur, adipisci ve
lit...",
        "createdBy" : ObjectId("5aafb06ec790687418346c68"),
        "lastUpdatedBy" : ObjectId("5aafb06ec790687418346c68"),
        "createdAt" : ISODate("2018-03-19T12:59:36.049Z"),
        "likes" : 0,
        "lastUpdateAt" : ISODate("2018-03-19T12:59:36.050Z"),
        "__v" : 0
}
rs-ds211309:PRIMARY> █
```

On the view thread page, the thread as well as the replies can be found and it should look something like this:

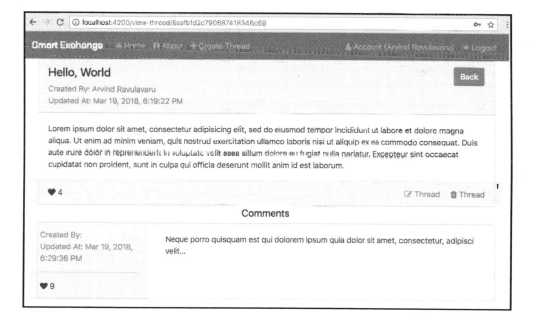

Simple right! Now the goal of our book is to make this application smarter while adding content to this forum. We will go through each of the Google Cloud AI services and then add one feature at a time to this application and make this forum app a smart forum app. Now that we have gone through the application, let's conclude this chapter by deploying the application to Heroku, so you can show off you new app!

Deploying to Heroku

This step is optional and you can do it if you are interested in deploying this application to Heroku. To continue with this section, you need to have set up a Heroku account and you need to have installed the Heroku Toolbelt.

1. Once that is done, open a new Command Prompt or Terminal inside the `smart-exchange-base` folder and run the following command:

   ```
   $ heroku login
   ```

   This is your prompt for your Heroku credentials that you have signed up with.

2. Once you are logged in, let's initialize a new git repository by using the following command:

   ```
   $ git init
   ```

3. Next, let's get our application ready for deployment. Run the following command:

   ```
   $ npm run build
   or
   $ yarn build
   ```

   This will run the required scripts to build the final `dist` folder, which will be deployed to Heroku. For everything to run smoothly on Heroku, we have added a file named `Procfile` that has the config that defines how our application needs to be invoked.

4. Once the build is completed, run the following command:

   ```
   $ git add -A
   $ git commit -am "Initial Commit"
   ```

5. Now we need to create our *Heroku* application. This is a one-time set up. Run the following command:

   ```
   $ heroku create smart-exchange
   ```

   In the above command `your-app-name` is the name of your app. I have chosen smart-exchange, you need to choose something different and available. If everything goes well, you should see that a new application has been created successfully and you should also see the *Heroku* application end point as well as the related git URL.

6. Now that the application is created, let's link that application to our application. This is also a one-time set up. Run the following command:

   ```
   $ heroku git:remote -a smart-exchange
   ```

7. Replace `smart-exchange` in the above command with your `app name`. This will link our local git to push to Heroku. Let's push the code to Heroku. Run the following command:

   ```
   $ git push heroku master
   ```

If everything goes well, the code will be uploaded to Heroku and you should be able to view the application at `https://smart-exchange.herokuapp.com` as shown in the following screenshot:

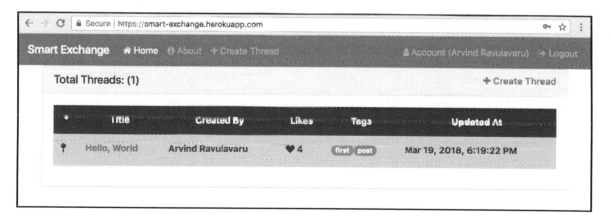

You can run `heroku open` command to launch the app.

Since the database is pointing to mLab, the application should show the same data that we have seen in our local development environment.

If you were using a local database for development, you need to point your application (update `MONGODB_URI`) to a public database details otherwise the application will fail to start.

This concludes the set up and deployment of the base application.

Summary

We started off this chapter by understanding the application architecture and the technology overview. Then, we installed the required dependencies and downloaded the base application. We then walked through the code and ran the application. Finally, we saw how to deploy the application to Heroku. In the next chapter, we will start interfacing with the first Google Cloud AI service Vision API and see how that can be used along with this application.

Cloud Vision API **3**

n the last chapter, we went through the high-level design of *SmartExchange*. We set up the local development environment and did a code walk-through. We also saw how to deploy the application to Heroku. In this chapter, we are going to integrate Google Cloud Vision API with *SmartExchange*. The topics covered are:

- What is Cloud Vision API?
- Exploring Cloud Vision API
- Integrating Cloud Vision API with *SmartExchange*

Cloud Vision API

Google Cloud Vision API is one of the machine learning services exposed under the Cloud AI vertical. This service is used to analyze images and their contents using machine learning models. This service can:

- Classify images into thousands of categories (label detection)
- Detect individual objects
- Detect faces
- Detect explicit content
- Detect logos
- Detect landmarks
- Detect similar images on the web (web detection)
- Get image attributes
- **OCR**: Optical Character Recognition

The beauty of Vision API is that it improves over time and continues to learn from various sources.

Pricing

You can read about the pricing here: `https://cloud.google.com/vision/#cloud-vision-api-pricing`.

Pricing is for 1,000 units and over a period of a month.

Example: If you apply face detection and label detection to the same image, each feature will be billed individually. You will be billed for 1 unit (1 API call) of label detection and 1 unit of face detection, at the price dictated by your monthly unit volume. If you use 4,300 units in a month of face detection, you will be billed as follows. You will be charged $0 for the first 1,000 units and for the remaining 3,300 units, you will be charged at $1.50 for every 1,000 units, rounded up to the next 1,000. So that would be 4 * $ 1.50 = $ 6. This should give you an idea of how you can keep an eye on your expenses.

Now that we know the basics of the Vision API and understand the pricing model, let's get started with a hands-on exploration. Before we get started, we need to set up the required authentication and authorization. In the next section, we are going to look at that.

When working with any Google Cloud AI service, we need to have either an API key or a service account key set up. Before we set up the API key or a service account, we need to have a Google project. If you already have a project, you can skip that section. Please refer to *Setting up an authentication* section from `Chapter 2`, *Setting Up a Smart Forum App*.

Enabling the API

Now that we have a project and we have both the API and service account keys, we will enable the required API and test our application:

1. Navigate to the project home page (`https://console.cloud.google.com/home/dashboard?project=smart-exchange-b10882`). From the menu on the left-hand side, select **APIs & Services | Library**.
2. Once we land on this page, search for **Vision API** and click on that card.

3. Then, click the **Enable** button. This will prompt you to set up billing as follows:

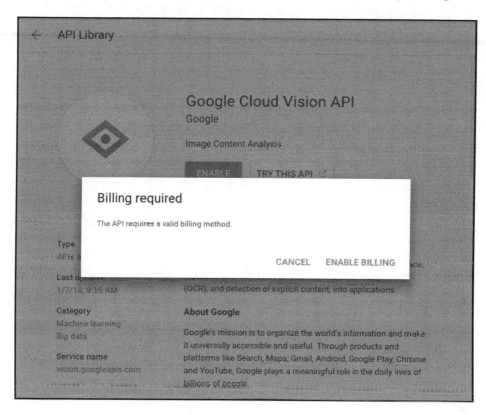

4. Click on **ENABLE BILLING**. You will be asked to select or create a new billing account:

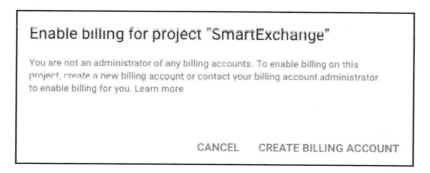

5. Click on **CREATE BILLING ACCOUNT**.

6. Fill in the form as shown on the following screens and validate your payment. Once that is done, you will be automatically redirected to the **Enable API** page and the API will be automatically enabled for you, if everything is set up correctly. Finally, you should see a screen as follows:

This concludes our section on enabling the API. In the next section, we are going to explore the API.

Setting up a REST client

Before we start exploring the APIs, we need a REST client to interface with these services. So, here are two REST clients and how you can set them up.

Setting up cURL

cURL is a command line tool for making HTTP requests. Since Cloud Vision API is accessed over REST, we can use curl as a client for it. You can download cURL for your OS from here: `https://curl.haxx.se/download.html`. You can test the installation by running the following command:

```
$ curl --version
```

```
curl 7.50.0 (x86_64-apple-darwin15.4.0) libcurl/7.50.0 OpenSSL/1.0.2h
zlib/1.2.8
Protocols: dict file ftp ftps gopher http https imap imaps pop3 pop3s rtsp
smb smbs smtp smtps telnet tftp
Features: IPv6 Largefile NTLM NTLM_WB SSL libz TLS-SRP UnixSockets
```

To test whether cURL is working as expected, run the following command:

```
$ curl https://reqres.in/api/users
```

This hits a public-hosted free mock REST API service named Req | Res (https://reqres.in/) and will return a bunch of users. Your output should look something like this:

```
//SNIPP SNIPP
{
    "page" : 1,
    "data" : [
        {
            "first_name" : "George",
            "avatar" :
"https://s3.amazonaws.com/uifaces/faces/twitter/calebogden/128.jpg",
            "id" : 1,
            "last_name" : "Bluth"
        },
        {
            "id" : 2,
            "avatar" :
"https://s3.amazonaws.com/uifaces/faces/twitter/josephstein/128.jpg",
            "last_name" : "Weaver",
            "first_name" : "Janet"
        },
        {
            "last_name" : "Wong",
            "id" : 3,
            "avatar" :
"https://s3.amazonaws.com/uifaces/faces/twitter/oleypogodaev/120.jpg",
            "first name" : "Emma"
        }
    ],
    "total_pages" : 4,
    "per_page" : 3,
    "total" : 12
}
//SNIPP SNIPP
```

If you are not comfortable with command line-based interaction, you can use a tool such as Postman.

Setting up Postman

Postman helps make HTTP requests with an intuitive UI. If you are not really a command-line person, you can use Postman for exploring REST APIs. You can download Postman from `https://www.getpostman.com/apps` or you can download the chrome extension from here: `https://chrome.google.com/webstore/detail/postman/fhbjgbiflinjbdggehcddcbncdddomop?hl=en`. Once you have installed Postman, you can launch it and sign up/log in if needed. Using the **New** menu on the top bar, click on **Request**. You will be asked to fill, a new request form; you can do so as shown here:

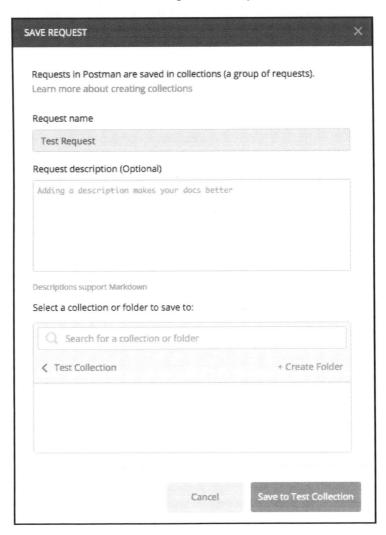

Now, create a new HTTP GET request pointing to `https://reqres.in/api/users` as shown here, click on **Send**, and you should see a response like this:

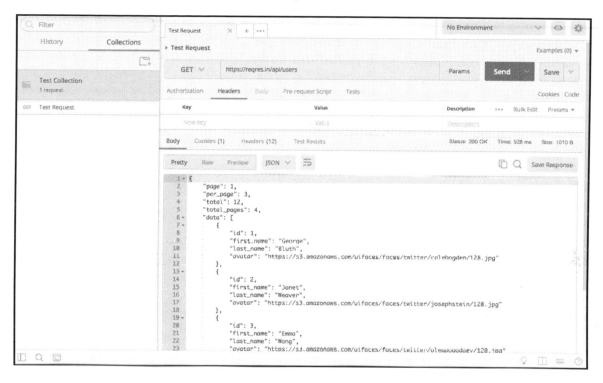

In this book, I am going to use Postman for making requests, primarily for ease of presentation. You can use any REST client you like.

Exploring the Vision API

Now that we have all the required setup done, let's get started with exploring the API. In this section, we are going to explore the following features of the Vision API:

- Face detection
- Label detection
- Safe search detection

We are going to explore these features using a REST API. There are other features as well, which are quite similar to those previously discussed. You can try them out for yourself.

Face detection

We are going to start off with face detection. In the `project` folder that you downloaded along with this book, or `https://github.com/PacktPublishing/Getting-Started-with-Google-Cloud-AI-Services`, you can find a folder for `Chapter 3`, inside that folder you will find another folder named `API`, and inside that folder, a folder named `Images`. Inside `Images`, I have placed all the sample image files that I have used for testing, for your reference. You are free to use any images.

Inside the `API\Image` folder, refer to the `Face_Detection_SriDevi.jpg` image. As a tribute to one of the greatest Indian actresses, I have used the picture of the late Sridevi Kapoor. The following is the image for reference:

Request structure

We are going to make a request as follows:

Field	Value
HTTP method	POST
URL	`https://vision.googleapis.com/v1/images:annotate?key=API_KEY`

Request body	<pre>// SNIPP SNIPP
{
"requests": [
{
"image": {
"content": "/9j/7QBEUGhvdG9zaG9...base64-encoded-image-
content...fXNWzvDEeYxxxzj/Coa6Bax//Z"
},
"features": [
{
"type": "FACE_DETECTION"
}
]
}
]
}
// SNIPP SNIPP</pre>

Note that the `content` property under the `image` property is the `base64` encoded version of the image. In the same `images` folder, you should find a file named `Face_Detection_SriDevi_base64.txt`. This is the `base64` version of the same image. You can use an online service such as `https://www.browserling.com/tools/image-to-base64` or `https://www.base64-image.de/` for converting your own image to a `base64` string. Under `features`, we are requesting the `FACE_DETECTION` feature.

 Neither Packt Publishing nor the author are endorsing the preceding links. Please use them at your own risk.

Constructing the request

Now, using Postman, we are going to construct a request and fire it at the Google Cloud Vision API. Click on the **New** option and then the **Request** option inside Postman.

Fill in the form shown here:

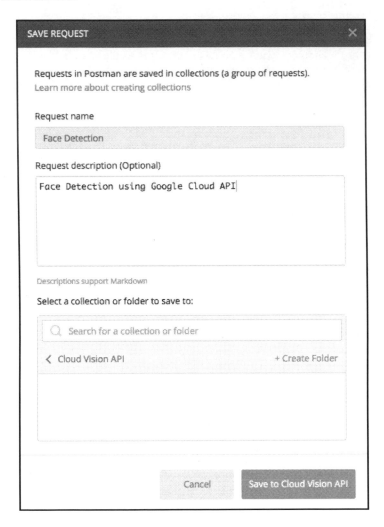

I have created a new collection named `Cloud Vision API` and placed this request inside that. You can import that collection into your Postman as well. This file is available in the `Chapter 3\API\Postman` folder. Update the new request as follows:

Field	Value
HTTP method	POST
URL	https://vision.googleapis.com/v1/images:annotate?key=API_KEY
Request body	```// SNIPP SNIPP
{
"requests": [
{
"image":
{
"content": "-- BASE64 ENCODED STRING ---"
},
"features": [
{
"type": "FACE_DETECTION"
}]
}]
}
// SNIPP SNIPP```

In the preceding fields, update the API key and `base64` encoded string, as applicable.

Analyzing the response

Now that we have built our request in Postman, click on **Send** and we should see something like this in Postman:

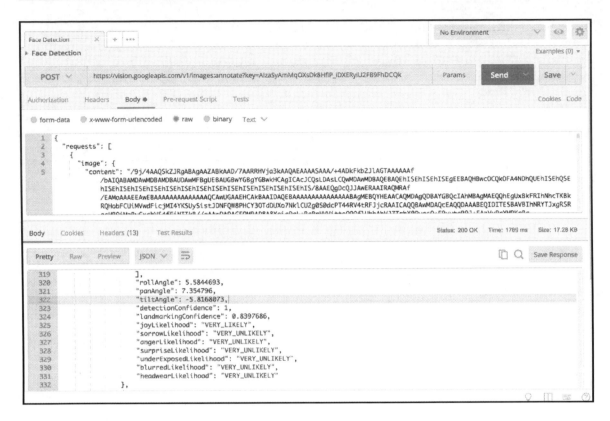

The response you have received should look something like this:

```
// SNIPP SNIPP
{
    "responses": [
        {
            "faceAnnotations": [
                {
                    "boundingPoly":
                    {
                        "vertices": [...]
                    },
                    "fdBoundingPoly":
                    {
                        "vertices": [...]
                    },
                    "landmarks": [
                        ...FACE FEATURES...
                    ],
                    "rollAngle": 5.5844693,
```

```
        "panAngle": 7.354796,
        "tiltAngle": -5.8168073,
        "detectionConfidence": 1,
        "landmarkingConfidence": 0.8397686,
        "joyLikelihood": "VERY_LIKELY",
        "sorrowLikelihood": "VERY_UNLIKELY",
        "angerLikelihood": "VERY_UNLIKELY",
        "surpriseLikelihood": "VERY_UNLIKELY",
        "underExposedLikelihood": "VERY_UNLIKELY",
        "blurredLikelihood": "VERY_UNLIKELY",
        "headwearLikelihood": "VERY_UNLIKELY"
      },
      // SNIPP SNIPP
    ]
  }]
}
// SNIPP SNIPP
```

I have removed a lot of information for brevity. As we can see from this, we have a lot of information regarding the image. The first thing I look for is `detectionConfidence`. It is a value between 0 and 1. A value of 1 indicates 100% confidence in the prediction. Next, let us have a look at the `boundingPoly` feature. This gives the bounds of the overall face, including any wearable, such as a hat. To validate the values from the response, I have taken the image, uploaded it to `http://resizeimage.net/`, and used their cropper tool to validate it. You can see the results:

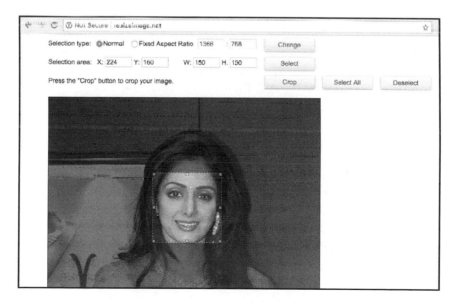

I have manually subtracted the left x point and right x point to get the width, and top y point and bottom y point to get the height. The next property is `fdBoundingPoly`. `fdBoundingPoly` is more a tighter boundary to the face, excluding the wearable. Here is the result:

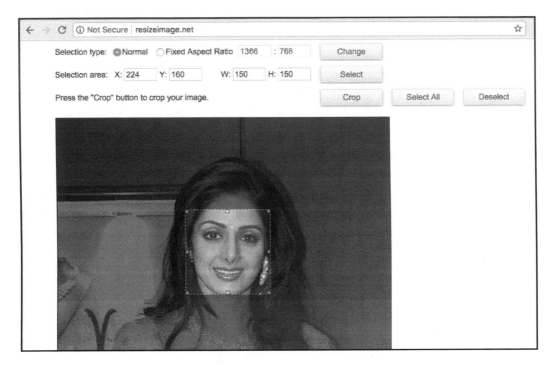

As you can see from this, `fdBoundingPoly` is the tighter bound image. Next, look at the following properties:

```
// SNIPP SNIPP
"rollAngle": 5.5844693,
"panAngle": 7.354796,
"tiltAngle": -5.8168073,
"detectionConfidence": 1,
"landmarkingConfidence": 0.8397686,
"joyLikelihood": "VERY_LIKELY",
"sorrowLikelihood": "VERY_UNLIKELY",
"angerLikelihood": "VERY_UNLIKELY",
"surpriseLikelihood": "VERY_UNLIKELY",
"underExposedLikelihood": "VERY_UNLIKELY",
"blurredLikelihood": "VERY_UNLIKELY",
"headwearLikelihood": "VERY_UNLIKELY"
// SNIPP SNIPP
```

joyLikelihood VERY_LIKELY is true, as we can see she is smiling. headwearLikelihood VERY_UNLIKELY, as she is not wearing a hat or a tiara. Pretty impressive, right? You can try a couple of images yourself and see how this works out.

You can find the reference for each property in the response object here: https://cloud. google.com/vision/docs/reference/rest/v1/images/annotate#FaceAnnotation. You can read more about Face Detection here: https://cloud.google.com/vision/docs/ detecting-faces and also how to use it with an SDK. Next, we are going to look at label detection.

Label detection

Label detection helps us understand the overall contents of the image. For this request, I am going to use this image by Min An: https://www.pexels.com/image/people-silhouette-during-sunset-853168/. You can find it in the API\Images folder with the name Label_Detection_pexels-image-853168.jpg and its corresponding base64 encoded image: Label_Detection_pexels-image-853168 base64.txt. This is the following image:

Request structure

We are going to make a request as follows:

Field	Value
HTTP method	POST
URL	https://vision.googleapis.com/v1/images:annotate?key=API_KEY

Request body	<code>// SNIPP SNIPP
	{
	   "requests": [
	    {
	      "image":
	      {
	        "content": "/9j/7QBEUGhvdG9zaG9...base64-encoded-image-content...fXNWzvDEeYxxxzj/Coa6Bax//Z"
	      },
	      "features": [
	      {
	        "type": "LABEL_DETECTION"
	      }]
	    }]
	}
	// SNIPP SNIPP</code>

Note that the content property under the `image` property is the `base64` encoded version of the image, and under the features, we are requesting the `LABEL_DETECTION` feature.

Constructing the request

Now, using Postman, we are going to construct a request and fire it to the Google Cloud Vision API. Click on **New** and then **Request** inside Postman. Fill in the form as applicable. I have created a new collection named `Cloud Vision API` and placed this request inside that. You can import that collection into your Postman as well. This file is available in the `Chapter 3\API\Postman` folder.

Update the new request as follows:

Field	Value
HTTP method	POST
URL	https://vision.googleapis.com/v1/images:annotate?key=API_KEY

Request body	<pre>// SNIPP SNIPP
	{
	    "requests": [
	        {
	            "image":
	            {
	                "content": "-- BASE64 ENCODED STRING ---"
	            },
	            "features": [
	                {
	                    "type": "LABEL_DETECTION"
	                }
	            ]
	        }
	    ]
	}
	// SNIPP SNIPP</pre>

In the preceding fields, update the API key and `base64` encoded string as applicable.

Analyzing the response

Now, click on **Send** and we should see something like this in Postman:

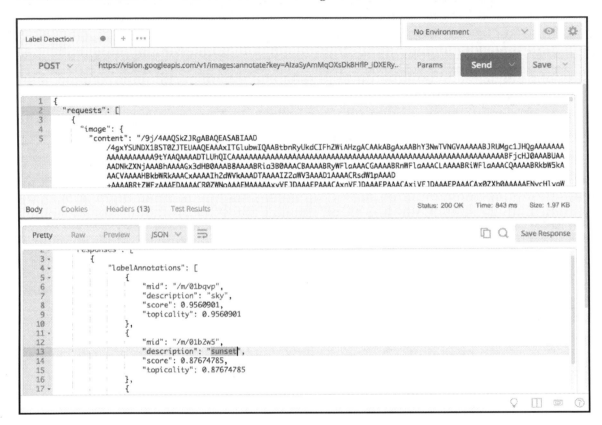

The response you have received should look something like this:

```
// SNIPP SNIPP
{
    "responses": [
    {
        "labelAnnotations": [
        {
            "mid": "/m/01bqvp",
            "description": "sky",
            "score": 0.9560901,
            "topicality": 0.9560901
        },
        {
            "mid": "/m/01b2w5",
```

```
        "description": "sunset",
        "score": 0.87674785,
        "topicality": 0.87674785
    },
    {
        "mid": "/m/06npx",
        "description": "sea",
        "score": 0.8571267,
        "topicality": 0.8571267
    },
    {
        "mid": "/m/01b2q6",
        "description": "sunrise",
        "score": 0.85168016,
        "topicality": 0.85168016
    },
    {
        "mid": "/m/0ds99lh",
        "description": "fun",
        "score": 0.791407,
        "topicality": 0.791407
    },
    {
        "mid": "/m/04mx32",
        "description": "evening",
        "score": 0.78113675,
        "topicality": 0.78113675
    },
    {
        "mid": "/m/06m_p",
        "description": "sun",
        "score": 0.7784385,
        "topicality": 0.7784385
    },
    {
        "mid": "/m/03thgk",
        "description": "silhouette",
        "score": 0.77650154,
        "topicality": 0.77650154
    },
    {
        "mid": "/m/0csby",
        "description": "cloud",
        "score": 0.77203345,
        "topicality": 0.77203345
    },
    {
        "mid": "/m/06z0n",
```

```
            "description": "sunlight",
            "score": 0.6308233,
            "topicality": 0.6308233
        }]
    }]
}
// SNIPP SNIPP
```

Most of the key components of the `image` are present, and the score indicates the confidence level of the prediction. You can read more about the properties of the response object here: `https://cloud.google.com/vision/docs/reference/rest/v1/images/annotate#EntityAnnotation`. Next, we are going to look at safe search detection.

Safe search detection

Safe search detection helps us in detecting whether the image that was uploaded has one or more of the following contents:

- Adult
- Spoof
- Medical
- Violence
- Racy

The image we are going to use for this example is of me smoking a pipe:

Request structure

We are going to make a request as follows:

Field	Value
HTTP method	POST
URL	https://vision.googleapis.com/v1/images:annotate?key=API_KEY
Request body	```// SNIPP SNIPP
{
"requests": [
{
"image":
{
"content": "/9j/7QDEUGhvdG9zaG9...base64-encoded-image-content...fXNWzvDEeYxxxzj/Coa6Bax//Z"
},
"features": [
{
"type": " SAFE_SEARCH_DETECTION"
}]
}]
}
// SNIPP SNIPP```

Note that the content property under the image property is the base64 encoded version of the image, and under the features, we are requesting the SAFE_SEARCH DETECTION feature.

Constructing the request

Now, we will create another request in Postman. Click on **New** and then **Request** inside Postman. Fill in the form as applicable. I have created a new collection named `Cloud Vision API` and placed this request inside that. You can import that collection into your Postman as well. This file is available in the `Chapter 3\API\Postman` folder. Update the new request as follows:

Field	Value
HTTP method	POST
URL	https://vision.googleapis.com/v1/images:annotate?key=API_KEY

Request body	`// SNIPP SNIPP`
	`{`
	`  "requests": [`
	`  {`
	`  "image":`
	`  {`
	`  "content": "-- BASE64 ENCODED STRING ---"`
	`  },`
	`  "features": [`
	`  {`
	`  "type": "SAFE_SEARCH_DETECTION"`
	`  }]`
	`  }]`
	`}`
	`// SNIPP SNIPP`

In the preceding fields, update the API key and `base64` encoded string, as applicable.

Analyzing the response

Now, click on **Send** and we should see something like this in Postman:

As we can see from the preceding response, the API thinks the image is a spoof. I am not sure what or whom I was spoofing. To understand more about the response object, refer to the safe search annotation: `https://cloud.google.com/vision/docs/reference/rest/v1/images/annotate#safesearchannotation`. There are other detections that are possible using the Cloud Vision API. You can explore other APIs here: `https://cloud.google.com/vision/docs/all-samples`. The process for exploring the APIs is the same as previously described.

API reference

You can find the reference for each property in the request object here: `https://cloud.google.com/vision/docs/reference/rest/v1/images/annotate#AnnotateImageRequest`.

- Face detection response: `https://cloud.google.com/vision/docs/reference/rest/v1/images/annotate#FaceAnnotation`
- Label detection response:
- `https://cloud.google.com/vision/docs/reference/rest/v1/images/annotate#EntityAnnotation`
- Safe search response: `https://cloud.google.com/vision/docs/reference/rest/v1/images/annotate#safesearchannotation`

Integrating Cloud Vision API with SmartExchange

Now that we have seen what can be done using Cloud Vision API, let's actually integrate this into *SmartExchange*. The idea is that we will allow users to upload images as part of their posts. Using the Cloud Vision API service, we are going to fetch the image labels, as well as checking the image for any explicit content using the label detection and safe search API.

The final output of the uploaded image and its contents will look like this:

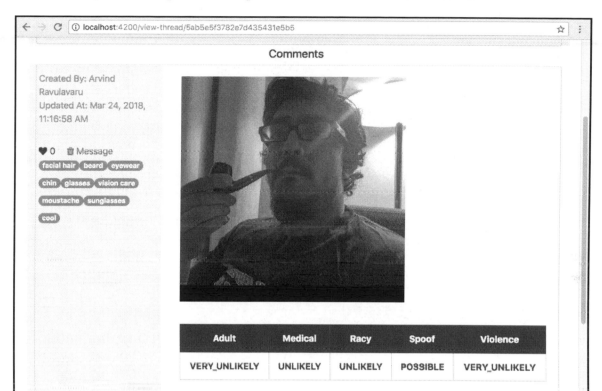

A simple and powerful way to protect the content on our sites, without any administration. So, let's get started with the implementation.

Solution design

To achieve the ability to screen images before we display them to the users on our application, we are going to do the following:

1. On the view-thread page, we are going to provide a button next to **Reply** named **Reply with Image** to keep things simple
2. The user is going to upload an image to our server using this interface
3. The image will be saved on our servers temporarily

4. The uploaded images will then be sent to the Google Cloud Vision API to detect labels and safe search annotations

5. If the safe search annotations return **POSSIBLE** for the adult, medical, or violence categories, we do not allow the user to upload the image

6. If the image is safe, we then upload it to Cloudinary, an image hosting service

7. Once the upload to Cloudinary is successful, we will get the public URL

8. Using all the data we have gathered so far, we are going to create a new message and then respond to it

9. The *Angular* app will process the response and update the thread

 Uploading images to Cloudinary is optional. I have implemented it to show an end-to-end flow.

Before we start the implementation, we need to create an API key for Cloudinary.

Setting up Cloudinary

Since we are going to host our images publicly, I have used a service named `Cloudinary` (`https://cloudinary.com/`). Cloudinary is an awesome platform for hosting images and video. The features they have are pretty good and are ideal for applications like *SmartExchange*.

Pricing

We are going to use the free plan for this book. But if you like this service, you can upgrade the plan. You can read more about Cloudinary pricing here: `https://cloudinary.com/pricing`.

API reference

We are going to use the Node.js SDK for our application. You can read more about the API reference here: `https://cloudinary.com/documentation/node_integration`. Here is the npm module that we are going to use: `https://www.npmjs.com/package/cloudinary`.

Signing up with Cloudinary

If you do not already have a Cloudinary account, you can head over to `https://cloudinary.com/users/register/free` and sign up. Verify your email to complete the process.

Managing the API key

Once you have successfully signed up and logged in, you should be taken to your dashboard. On your dashboard, in the **Account Details** section, you will find your **Cloud name**, **API Key**, and **API Secret**, as follows:

Open your `.env` file placed at the root of the *SmartExchange* code and add the following three lines:

```
// SNIPP SNIPP
CLOUDINARY_CLOUD_NAME=dp1xngshs
CLOUDINARY_API_KEY=8941474971477
CLOUDINARY_API_SECRET=hcwmjJZuKHEfmz6fd-PiSnZE
// SNIPP SNIPP
```

Update the values as applicable. Save the file and we will come back to these variables when we are implementing uploads to Cloudinary.

Setting up the server code

Now that we have our Cloudinary account set up, we will continue. Open your `.env` file placed at the root of the *SmartExchange* code and add the following:

```
// SNIPP SNIPP
GCP_API_KEY=AIzaSyAmMqOXsDk8HflP_iDXERyiU2FB9FhDCQk
// SNIPP SNIPP
```

This is the API key that we used earlier to make a request to the Google Cloud Vision API. We are going to use it programmatically.

Installing dependencies

For handling file uploads, we are going to use a module named multer (https://www.npmjs.com/package/multer), and for managing file uploads to Cloudinary, we are going to use an npm named Cloudinary (https://www.npmjs.com/package/cloudinary). We are also going to use an npm named request (https://www.npmjs.com/package/request) for making HTTP calls from Node.js. Run the following command from the root of the application:

```
$ npm install --save cloudinary multer request
```

Or, you can run the following command instead:

```
$ yarn add cloudinary multer request
```

Defining routes

Now that we have the required dependencies, we will add the routes. Inside the server\routes folder, create a file named cloud-ai-api.ts and update it as follows:

```
// SNIPP SNIPP
import * as express from 'express';
import * as multer from 'multer';

const UPLOAD_PATH = __dirname + '/../uploads';
const upload = multer({ dest: `${UPLOAD_PATH}/` });

import { Authenticate, Authorize } from '../auth';

import VisionAPI from '../controllers/cloud-ai-api';

export default function defineCloudAIAPIRoutes(app) {
    const router = express.Router();
    const visionAPI = new VisionAPI();

    // Upload Single Images
    router.post('/upload-image/:threadId', Authenticate,
Authorize('user'), upload.single('image-reply'), visionAPI.uploadImage);

    // Apply the routes to our application with the prefix /api
    app.use('/api', router);
}
// SNIPP SNIPP
```

Here, we have one post route, which accepts an image with a form name of `image-reply` and forwards that image to `visionAPI.checkImage()`. Now, we are going to add this route to the list of routes we already have. Update `server\routes.ts` as follows:

```
// SNIPP SNIPP
import * as express from 'express';
import defineUserRoutes from './routes/user';
import defineThreadRoutes from './routes/thread';
import defineMessageRoutes from './routes/message';
import defineCloudAIAPIRoutes from './routes/cloud-ai-api';

export default function setRoutes(app) {
  const router = express.Router();

  defineUserRoutes(app);
  defineThreadRoutes(app);
  defineMessageRoutes(app);
  defineCloudAIAPIRoutes(app);
}
// SNIPP SNIPP
```

Updating the message model

Next, we are going to update our message model. We are going to save the labels, safe search result, and Cloudinary upload details, as well in the message. These values will be populated only for an image upload and not a text upload.
Update `server\models\message.ts` as follows:

```
// SNIPP SNIPP
import * as mongoose from 'mongoose';
const Schema = mongoose.Schema;

const messageSchema = new Schema({
    // SNIPP SNIPP
    labels: [{
        type: Schema.Types.Mixed,
        default: []
    }],
    cloudinaryProps: {
        type: Schema.Types.Mixed
    },
    safeSearchProps: {
        type: Schema.Types.Mixed
    }
});
```

```
const Message = mongoose.model('Message', messageSchema);

export default Message;
// SNIPP SNIPP
```

Defining the controller

Now that are done with defining the routes and updating the model, we will work on the logic discussed in the *Solution design* section earlier. Create a new file named `cloud-ai-api.ts` inside the `server/controllers` folder. First, we will add the required imports and configure the Cloudinary client as follows:

```
// SNIPP SNIPP
import * as request from 'request';
import * as fs from 'fs';
import * as dotenv from 'dotenv';
import * as cloudinary from 'cloudinary';

import Message from '../models/message';

dotenv.config();

const API_KEY = process.env.GCP_API_KEY;

cloudinary.config({
    cloud_name: process.env.CLOUDINARY_CLOUD_NAME,
    api_key: process.env.CLOUDINARY_API_KEY,
    api_secret: process.env.CLOUDINARY_API_SECRET
});
// SNIPP SNIPP
```

Next, we are going to implement the `VisionAPI` class with a `respondErrorMessage` helper:

```
// SNIPP SNIPP
export default class VisionAPI {
    respondErrorMessage = (res, err) => {
        return res.status(500).json(err);
    }
  // SNIPP
```

Next, we are going to define the `uploadImage` method:

```
// SNIPP SNIPP
uploadImage = (req, res) => {
        // console.log('req.file', req.file);
```

```
        const filePath = req.file.path;
        this.base64_encode(filePath).then((BASE64_CONTENT) => {
                const formData = JSON.stringify({
                        'requests': [
                                {
                                        'image': {
                                                'content': BASE64_CONTENT
                                        },
                                        'features': [
                                                {
                                                        'type':
'LABEL_DETECTION'
                                                }, {
                                                        'type':
'SAFE_SEARCH_DETECTION'
                                                }
                                        ]
                                }
                        ]
        });
        var options = {
                method: 'POST',
                url: 'https://vision.googleapis.com/v1/images:annotate',
                qs: {
                        key: `${API_KEY}`
                },
                body: formData
        };

        request(options, (error, response, body) => {
                if (error) {
                        // Delete the local file so we don't clutter

                        this.deleteFile(filePath);
                        return this.respondErrorMessage(res, error);
                }

                let results = this.getJSONObject(body);
                if (!results) {
                        // Delete the local file so we don't clutter

                        this.deleteFile(filePath);
                        return this.respondErrorMessage(res, { 'message':
'Invalid Response from Google Cloud Vision API' });
                }
                results = results.responses;

                let labelAnnotations = results[0].labelAnnotations;
```

```
            let safeSearchAnnotations =
results[0].safeSearchAnnotation;

            if (safeSearchAnnotations.adult === 'POSSIBLE') {
                // Delete the local file so we don't clutter

                this.deleteFile(filePath);
                return res.status(400).json({
                    message: 'Adult Content is not allowed'
                })
            }
            if (safeSearchAnnotations.medical === 'POSSIBLE') {

                // Delete the local file so we don't clutter

                this.deleteFile(filePath);
                return res.status(400).json({
                    message: 'Medical Content'
                })
            }
            if (safeSearchAnnotations.violence === 'POSSIBLE') {

                // Delete the local file so we don't clutter

                this.deleteFile(filePath);
                return res.status(400).json({
                    message: 'Violence Content violence'
                })
            }
            let msg = new Message();
            msg.thread = req.params.threadId;
            msg.createdBy = req.user;
            msg.lastUpdatedBy = req.user;
            msg.labels = labelAnnotations;
            msg.safeSearchProps = safeSearchAnnotations;

            // Upload our image to cloudinary for external file
hosting

            // This is optional & you can use any service for the same

            cloudinary.uploader.upload(filePath, (result) => {
                // Delete the local file so we don't clutter

                this.deleteFile(filePath);
                if (result.error) {
                    return res.status(400).json({
                        message: result.error.message
```

```
                                        });
                                }
                                msg.cloudinaryProps = result;
                                msg.description = `<img style="max-width:80%;
height:auto;" src="${result.secure_url}"
alt="${result.original_filename}">`

                                msg.save((err, msg) => {
                                        if (err) {
                                                return this.respondErrorMessage(res,
err);
                                        }
                                        res.status(200).json(msg);
                                });
                        });
                });
        });
    }
// SNIPP SNIPP
```

In the preceding method, we first extract the `filePath` from `req.file` and get the image we are trying to process. Using `base64_encode()`, we convert the image to a `base64` encoded string programmatically. Next, we construct the request payload for sending this image to the Google Cloud Vision API. Using the request module, we are going to send the payload with our API key to get the results.

Once the results arrive, we extract `labelAnnotations` and `safeSearchAnnotations`, and check whether `safeSearchAnnotations` has a high possibility of adult, medical, or violence categories. If everything is good, we are going to upload the validated image to Cloudinary, and then save all the data we have gathered so far as a message and respond with the newly created message document. Finally, here are the three helper methods:

```
//SNIPP SNIPP
base64_encode    (filePath) -> {
    return new Promise((res, rej) => {
        try {
            // read binary data
            const bitmap = fs.readFileSync(filePath);
            // convert binary data to base64 encoded string
            const base64String = new Buffer(bitmap).toString('base64');
            res(base64String);
        } catch (e) {
            rej(e);
        }
    });
}
```

```
getJSONObject = (jsonStr) => {
    try {
        return JSON.parse(jsonStr);
    } catch (ex) {
        return false;
    }
}
deleteFile = (filePath: string) => {
    fs.unlink(filePath);
}
// SNIPP SNIPP
```

This wraps up our controller logic, as well as our service-side logic. In the next section, we are going to work on the client-side logic.

Setting up the client code

We are going to get started by adding a dependency named ng-bootstrap (https://ng-bootstrap.github.io/#/components/modal/examples). ng-bootstrap provides Bootstrap 4 components the angular way.

Setting up the ng-bootstrap

In the Command Prompt or Terminal pointing at the application root folder, run the following command to install dependencies:

```
$ npm install --save @ng-bootstrap/ng-bootstrap
```

Or you can use this:

```
$ yarn add @ng-bootstrap/ng-bootstrap
```

Next, we need to import the NgbModule into our *Angular* application. Open client\app\app.module.ts and add the following import:

```
// SNIPP SNIPP
import { NgbModule } from '@ng-bootstrap/ng-bootstrap';

// SNIPP SNIPP
```

And then update imports as follows:

```
// SNIPP SNIPP
imports: [
```

```
        BrowserModule,
        RoutingModule,
        SharedModule,
        FormsModule,
        HttpClientModule,
        NgxEditorModule,
        TagsInputModule.forRoot(),
        NgbModule.forRoot()
    ],
    // SNIPP SNIPP
```

This concludes setting up ng-bootstrap.

Modifying the view thread component

I wanted to keep the image upload feature simple. So, along with the existing reply with text features, we are going to add another button named **Reply with Image**. This button will launch a modal and help us with the upload process. Open client\app\view-thread\view-thread.component.html and next to the **Reply** button at the bottom of the page, add the following code:

```
// SNIPP SNIPP
<div class="col text-center">
            <button class="btn btn-info" type="submit"
(click)="uploadImage(thread)"><i class="fa fa-user-plus"></i> Reply with
Image</button>
        </div>
// SNIPP SNIPP
```

Next, the required logic for uploadImage will be placed in client\app\view-thread\view-thread.component.ts and should be as follows:

```
// SNIPP SNIPP
uploadImage(thread: Thread) {
        const modalRef = this.modal.open(UploadImageModal);
        modalRef.componentInstance.threadId = this.thread._id;
        modalRef.componentInstance.updateThread.subscribe((message) -> {
                if (!message) return;
                thread.messages.push(message);
        });
}
// SNIPP SNIPP
```

Here, we are using the `NgbModal` instance to open the upload image component, which we are going to create in a moment. Using the `componentInstance` on `modalRef`, we are sending the thread ID to that component. We will be creating an output named `updateThread` on the upload image component and subscribing to that event. `updateThread` sends back the newly created message to be added to the existing list of messages in the thread. Add the following two imports to `client\app\view-thread\view-thread.component.ts`:

```
// SNIPP SNIPP
import { UploadImageModal } from './upload-image-modal/upload-image-modal';
import { NgbModal } from '@ng-bootstrap/ng-bootstrap';
// SNIPP SNIPP
```

And update the view thread component constructor as follows:

```
// SNIPP SNIPP
constructor(
 public auth: AuthService,
 public toast: ToastComponent,
 private router: Router,
 private route: ActivatedRoute,
 private formBuilder: FormBuilder,
 private threadService: ThreadService,
 private messageService: MessageService,
 private modal: NgbModal
) {}
// SNIPP SNIPP
```

Now, we will create the upload image modal component.

Setting up the upload image modal component

Inside the `client\app\view-thread` folder, create another folder named `upload-image-modal` and inside that, create two files named `upload-image-modal.html` and `upload-image-modal.ts`. Update `client\app\view-thread\upload-image-modal\upload-image-modal.html` as follows:

```
// SNIPP SNIPP
<div class="modal-header">
    <h4 class="modal-title">Reply with Image</h4>
    <button type="button" class="close" aria-label="Close"
(click)="activeModal.dismiss('x')">
        <span aria-hidden="true">&times;</span>
    </button>
```

```
</div>
<div class="modal-body">
    <div class="form-group">
        <input type="file" id="file"
(change)="handleFileInput($event.target.files)">
        <p class="text-center mt-5 mb-0">
            <img [src]="filePreviewPath" width="200"
*ngIf="filePreviewPath" />
        </p>
        <p>
            <br>
            <ngb-alert [dismissible]="false" *ngIf="invalidImage">
                <strong>Warning!</strong> Please upload a valid image file.
Supported file types are {{AllowedImageExt.join(',')}}
            </ngb-alert>
            <br>
            <ngb-alert [dismissible]="false" *ngIf="largeFile">
                <strong>Warning!</strong> Max file size: 2MB. Uploaded file
size {{getFileSize()}}
            </ngb-alert>
        </p>
    </div>
    <ngb-alert type="danger" [dismissible]="false" *ngIf="error">
        <strong>Error!</strong> {{error.message || error}}
    </ngb-alert>
</div>
<div class="modal-footer">
    <i *ngIf="isProcessing" class="fa fa-circle-o-notch fa-spin fa-3x"></i>
    <button type="button" class="btn btn-success" [disabled]="isProcessing
|| !fileToUpload || invalidImage || largeFile"
(click)="reply()">Reply</button>
</div>
// SNIPP SNIPP
```

Here, we have a file uploader and an image tag for an image preview. Apart from that, we have the required error messages and loading indicators. For the required logic, we will get started by adding the imports to client\app/view-thread/upload-image-modal\upload-image-modal.ts:

```
// SNIPP SNIPP
import { Component, Input, Output, EventEmitter } from '@angular/core';
import { NgbActiveModal } from '@ng-bootstrap/ng-bootstrap';
import { ActivatedRoute } from '@angular/router';
import { DomSanitizer, SafeUrl } from '@angular/platform-browser';
import { VisionAPIService } from '../../services/vision.api.service';

import { GLOBAL } from '../../services/global.constants';
```

```
import { HELPER } from '../../services/helpers.global';
// SNIPP SNIPP
```

We are going to create the missing dependencies in a moment. Next, we are going to define the `UploadImageModal` component as follows:

```
// SNIPP SNIPP
@Component({
        selector: 'sm-create-asset-modal',
        templateUrl: './upload-image-modal.html'
})
export class UploadImageModal {
        fileToUpload: File = null;
        invalidImage: boolean = false;
        largeFile: boolean = false;
        isProcessing: boolean = false;
        AllowedImageExt: Array < string > = GLOBAL.allowedImageExt;
        @Input() threadId; // fetch from view-thread page
        @Output() updateThread = new EventEmitter < any > (); // Update
main thread with new message
        error: string = '';
        filePreviewPath: SafeUrl;
}
// SNIPP SNIPP
```

The constructor will be as follows:

```
// SNIPP SNIPP
constructor(
        public activeModal: NgbActiveModal,
        public visionAPIService: VisionAPIService,
        private route: ActivatedRoute,
        private sanitizer: DomSanitizer
) {}
// SNIPP SNIPP
```

We have `handleFileInput ()`, which gets triggered when a new file is selected:

```
// SNIPP SNIPP
handleFileInput(files: FileList) {
        this.fileToUpload = files.item(0);
        if (!this.fileToUpload) return; // when user escapes the file
picker
        if (this.fileToUpload.size > 2000000) { // 2MB max file size
                this.largeFile = true;
        } else {
                this.largeFile = false;
        }
```

```
        if (!this.isValidFileType(this.fileToUpload.name)) {
                this.invalidImage = true;
        } else {
                this.invalidImage = false;
        }
        if (!this.invalidImage && !this.largeFile) {
                this.filePreviewPath
=this.sanitizer.bypassSecurityTrustUrl((window.URL.createObjectURL(this.fil
eToUpload)));
        }
}
// SNIPP SNIPP
```

As we can see from this, we are going to validate that the uploaded file is an image, as well as ensure the image size does not exceed 2 MB. Then, using `sanitizer.bypassSecurityTrustUrl`, we create a temp URL for the image file to be shown in the preview. Next is the `reply` method that posts data to our server and updates the view thread component with the newly created message:

```
// SNIPP SNIPP
reply() {
        this.isProcessing = true;
        this.visionAPIService.postFile(this.threadId,
this.fileToUpload).subscribe(data => {
        console.log(data);
        this.updateThread.emit(data);
        this.isProcessing = false;
        this.activeModal.close();
  }, error => {
        console.log(error);
        this.error - error;
        this.isProcessing = false;
    });
}
// SNIPP SNIPP
```

Finally, we have a couple of helpers, as follows:

```
// SNIPP SNIPP
getFileSize(): string {
  return HELPER.getFileSize(this.fileToUpload.size, 0);
}

private isValidFileType(fName) {
  return this.AllowedImageExt.indexOf(fName.split('.').pop()) > -1;
}
// SNIPP SNIPP
```

This concludes our upload image modal component. Before we proceed, we need to add this component to `client\app\app.module.ts`. First, let's import `UploadImageModal` into `client\app\app.module.ts`:

```
// SNIPP SNIPP
import { UploadImageModal } from './view-thread/upload-image-modal/upload-
image-modal';
// SNIPP SNIPP
```

Next, we will add this modal to `declarations` as well as `entryComponents`, as follows:

```
// SNIPP SNIPP
declarations: [
        AppComponent,
        AboutComponent,
        RegisterComponent,
        LoginComponent,
        LogoutComponent,
        AccountComponent,
        AdminComponent,
        NotFoundComponent,
        HomeComponent,
        CreateThreadComponent,
        ViewThreadComponent,
        FilterThreadPipe,
        EditThreadComponent,
        UploadImageModal
    ],
    entryComponents: [
        UploadImageModal
    ],
// SNIPP SNIPP
```

Save all the files and we are good to move on. Now, we will fill in the missing dependencies.

Completing the view thread component

Now that we have the upload image component done, we will complete minor UI changes to the view thread page, which will present the data we have gathered in a better way. Open `client\app\view-thread\view-thread.component.html` and update the card, which displays the message as follows:

```
// SNIPP SNIPP
<div class="card mb-2" *ngFor="let message of thread.messages">
```

```
    <div class="row">
        <div class="col-3 card-header">
            <p>Created By: {{message.createdBy.name}}</p>
            <p>Updated At: {{message.lastUpdateAt | date:'medium'}}</p>
            <hr>
            <span class="pointer" (click)="incMessageLikes(message)">
                    <i class="fa fas fa-heart"></i> {{message.likes}}
                </span>
            <span class="text-danger pointer"
*ngIf="auth.getCurrentUser()._id === message.createdBy._id ||
auth.getCurrentUser().role === 'admin'" (click)="deleteMessage(message)">
                    <i class="fa fas fa-trash"></i> Message
                </span>
            <br>
            <label class="badge badge-pill badge-info" *ngFor="let l of
message.labels">
                    {{l.description}}
            </label>
        </div>
    <div class="col">
        <div class="card-body">
            <p class="card-text"
[innerHTML]="sanitizeContent(message.description)"></p>
            <br>
            <div class="table-responsive" *ngIf="message.safeSearchProps">
                <table class="table table-bordered">
                    <thead class="thead-dark text-center">
                        <tr>
                            <th scope="col">Adult</th>
                            <th scope="col">Medical</th>
                            <th scope="col">Racy</th>
                            <th scope="col">Spoof</th>
                            <th scope="col">Violence</th>
                        </tr>
                    </thead>
                <tbody>
                    <tr class="text-center">
                        <th>
                            {{message.safeSearchProps.adult}}
                        </th>
                        <th>
                            {{message.safeSearchProps.medical}}
                        </th>
                        <th>
                            {{message.safeSearchProps.racy}}
                        </th>
                        <th>
                            {{message.safeSearchProps.spoof}}
```

```
                              </th>
                              <th>
                                  {{message.safeSearchProps.violence}}
                              </th>
                          </tr>
                      </tbody>
                  </table>
              </div>
            </div>
          </div>
        </div>
      </div>
    <br>
// SNIPP SNIPP
```

In the preceding code snippet, we are displaying the image and its properties in a more presentable format. To complete the component, we will add the `sanitizeContent` helper to our `client\app\view-thread\view-thread.component.ts`:

```
// SNIPP SNIPP
sanitizeContent(content: string) {
 return this.sanitizer.bypassSecurityTrustHtml(content);
}
// SNIPP SNIPP
```

Then, update the constructor as follows:

```
// SNIPP SNIPP
constructor(
 public auth: AuthService,
 public toast: ToastComponent,
 private router: Router,
 private route: ActivatedRoute,
 private formBuilder: FormBuilder,
 private threadService: ThreadService,
 private messageService: MessageService,
 private modal: NgbModal,
 private sanitizer: DomSanitizer
) {}
// SNIPP SNIPP
```

Follow this by adding the required import:

```
// SNIPP SNIPP
import { DomSanitizer } from '@angular/platform-browser';
// SNIPP SNIPP
```

sanitizeContent() will tell the renderer that the content we are trying to inject is safe. You can read more about it here: https://angular.io/guide/security. Save all the files to move on.

Creating the Vision API service

To upload the image to our server, we are using postFile() on VisionAPIService. Let's create this service now. Inside the client\app\services folder, create a file named vision.api.service.ts and update it as follows:

```
// SNIPP SNIPP
import { Injectable } from '@angular/core';
import { HttpClient } from '@angular/common/http';
import { Observable } from 'rxjs/Observable';

@Injectable()
export class VisionAPIService {

        constructor(private http: HttpClient) {}

        postFile(threadId: string, fileToUpload: File): Observable < any >
{
            const formData: FormData = new FormData();
            formData.append('image-reply', fileToUpload,
fileToUpload.name);
            return this.http.post < any > (`/api/upload-
image/${threadId}`, formData);
        }
}
// SNIPP SNIPP
```

We need to add this service as a provider in client\app\app.module.ts. First, we will import VisionAPIService into client\app\app.module.ts:

```
// SNIPP SNIPP
import { VisionAPIService } from './services/vision.api.service';
// SNIPP SNIPP
```

Update the providers as follows:

```
// SNIPP SNIPP
providers: [
    AuthService,
    AuthGuardLogin,
    AuthGuardAdmin,
```

```
        UserService,
        ThreadService,
        MessageService,
        VisionAPIService,
        {
            provide: HTTP_INTERCEPTORS,
            useClass: TokenInterceptor,
            multi: true
        }
    ],
    // SNIPP SNIPP
```

Save all the files to continue.

Managing the helpers

Inside the `client\app\services` folder, create a file named `helpers.global.ts` and update it as follows:

```
// SNIPP SNIPP
export const HELPER = {
getFileSize: function(bytes: number, decimals ? : number): string {
            if (bytes == 0) return '0 Bytes';
            var k = 1024,
                dm = decimals || 2,
                sizes = ['Bytes', 'KB', 'MB', 'GB', 'TB', 'PB', 'EB',
'ZB', 'YB'],
                i = Math.floor(Math.log(bytes) / Math.log(k));
            return parseFloat((bytes / Math.pow(k, i)).toFixed(dm)) + ' '
+ sizes[i];
    }
}
// SNIPP SNIPP
```

As of now, we have one helper method, which converts bytes to human readable file sizes. Next, update `client\app\services\global.constants.ts` and add the following:

```
// SNIPP SNIPP
export const GLOBAL = {
        // SNIPP
        allowedImageExt: ['jpg', 'jpeg', 'gif', 'bmp', 'png']
}
// SNIPP SNIPP
```

That is it; these are all the changes needed to test out our Vision API integration with *SmartExchange*.

Testing the app

Make sure you have updated the code as previously detailed and installed the required dependencies before going forward. To test the app, from the root of the `application` folder, run:

```
$ npm run dev
```

Or run this:

```
$ yarn dev
```

This will launch our application. From the home page, click on **Create New Thread** and create a new thread named **Vision API Test**, or any name you want:

Once we create a new thread and navigate to the view thread page, we should see the new reply section:

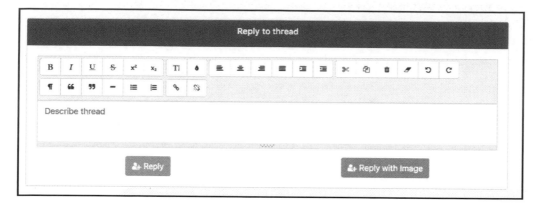

When we click on **Reply with Image**, we should see a popup where you can upload an image. If the image is valid and under 2 MB, we should see a preview:

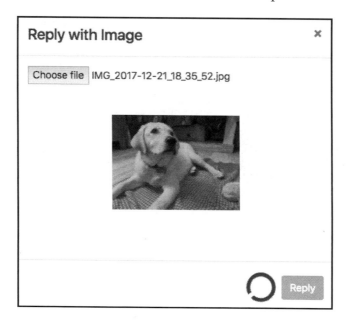

This handsome guy is Dexter. Now, when we click on **Reply**, the image will get uploaded to our server first, and then it will upload the same image to Cloud Vision API to get the labels and safe search annotations. If everything is as expected, this image will be uploaded to Cloudinary, a public URL of this image is fetched, and the description for this image is constructed and sent back. And this is how the final message will look:

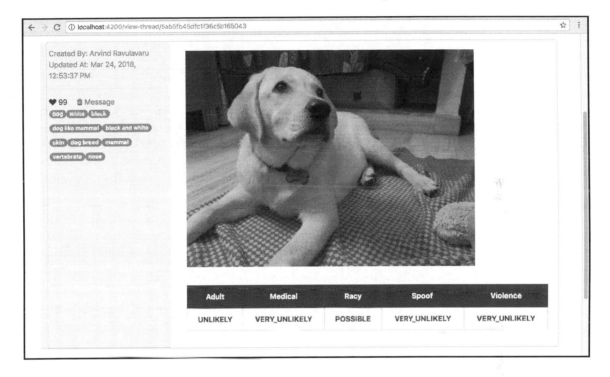

The labels appear on the left side and the safe search information below the image. Here is the image from Pexels, `https://www.pexels.com/image/alphabets-camera-card-desk-407294/`, and the results are as follows:

You can try uploading various images and test the complete flow end to end.

 Keep an eye on the number of API requests you are making to the Cloud Vision API as well as Cloudinary.

To wrap up this chapter, we are going to push the code to Heroku.

Deploying to Heroku

This step is optional and you can do it if you are interested in deploying this app to Heroku. To continue with this section, you need to have set up a Heroku account and installed the Heroku Toolbelt. Once that is done, open a new Command Prompt or Terminal inside the `smart-exchange-base` folder, and then run:

```
$ heroku login
```

This will prompt for the Heroku credentials that you signed up with. Next, let's get our application ready for deployment. Run this:

```
$ npm run build
```

Or run this:

```
$ yarn build
```

This will run the scripts required to build the final `dist` folder, which will be deployed to Heroku. Once the build is completed, run the following:

```
$ git add -A
$ git commit -am "Vision API Integration Commit"
```

Let's push the code to Heroku. Run this:

```
$ git push heroku master
```

If everything goes well, the code will be uploaded to Heroku and you should be able to view the application at `https://smart-exchange.herokuapp.com`, as follows:

Summary

In this chapter, we went through the Google Cloud Vision API and worked with three features of the API. Then, we set up the required code to integrate this API with the *SmartExchange* app. In the next chapter, we are going to work with the Video Intelligence API.

Video Intelligence API
4

In the last chapter, we saw how to work with the Cloud Vision API. We then learned how to integrate this API with *SmartExchange* and get labels from the uploaded images, as well as administer an image before posting it as. Reply to a thread using Safe Search Annotations.. In this chapter, we are going to work with Video Intelligence API. We are going to let a user record a video from the app, and post it. Behind the scenes, we are going to upload this video to Video Intelligence API and get labels, as well as detect any explicit content. If the video is acceptable as per our forum guidelines, we post the video, else we reject the video.

The topics covered are:

- What is Video Intelligence API?
- Exploring Video Intelligence API
- Integrating Video Intelligence API with *SmartExchange*

Video Intelligence API

Google Video Intelligence API is one of the machine learning services exposed under the Cloud AI vertical. This service is used to analyze a video and its contents using machine learning models.

This service can:

- Gather insights from 20,000 labels
- Search video catalogues
- Distinguish scenes using shot detection

Some of the best use cases for this API are:

- Content recommendation
- Content moderation
- Contextual advertisements
- Searchable media archives

Using this API, we can detect the following:

- **Label detection**: From a given video, identify various items/things present in the video
- **Explicit Content Detection**: Detect adult content in a video, along with the position of occurance
- **Shot Change detection**: Detect scene changes in a video
- **Video Transcription** [ALPHA]: Transcribe the video content into English

Pricing

The pricing for this service is as follows:

Feature	Pricing
Label detection	Free till 1,000 minutes and $0.10/minute till 100,000 minutes
Shot detection	Free till 1,000 minutes and $0.05/minute till 100,000 minutes, or free with label detection

You can read more about pricing here: https://cloud.google.com/video-intelligence/#cloud-video-intelligence-pricing.

Now that we have the basics of the Video Intelligence API and understand the pricing model, let's get started with hands-on exploration.

Before we get started, we need to set up the required authentication and authorization. In the next section, we are going to look at that.

When working with any Google Cloud AI service, we need to have either an API key or a service account key set up. Before we set up the API key or a service account, we need to have a Google Cloud project. If you already have a project, you can skip that section. Please refer to *Setting up an authentication* section from Chapter 2, *Setting Up a Smart Forum App.*

Enabling API

Now that we have a project, and we have both API and service account keys, we will enable the required API and test our application. Navigate to the project home page (`https://console.cloud.google.com/home/dashboard?project=smart-exchange-b10882`). From the menu on the left-hand side, select **APIs & Services | Library**. Once we land on this page, search for **Video Intelligence API** and click on that card. Then, click on the **Enable** button. Your Enable API screen after enabling should look like this:

If you have not set up billing, you will be prompted to first set up billing before you continue.

This concludes our section on enabling the API. In the next section, we are going to explore the API.

Exploring Video Intelligence API

Please refer to the *Setting up a Rest Client* Section from `Chapter 3`, *Cloud Vision API* to set up a REST API client, before you continue. Now that we have all the required setup done, let's get started with exploring the API. In this section, we are going to explore only the label detection feature using REST API. You can explore other features by yourself in a similar fashion.

Label detection

We are going to start off with label detection. In the project folder that you downloaded along with this book (or you can download the same from `https://github.com/PacktPublishing/Getting-Started-with-Google-Cloud-AI-Services`) you will find a folder named `Chapter 4` ; inside that folder you will find another folder named `API`, and inside that folder a folder named `Videos`. Inside the `Videos` folder, I have placed all the sample image files that I have used for testing, for your reference. You are free to use any videos. In the `API\Videos` folder, refer to the video called `Label_Detection_Pexels_Video_699572008.webm`. Here is a screenshot of one of the frames of the video, for your reference:

Source: `https://videos.pexels.com/videos/close-up-video-of-a-woman-studying-855418`.

This is a video of a girl reading a book. To work with any Video Intelligence API, we need to make two requests. Since video analysis cannot happen on the fly (at least not today), we need to first make a request, submitting the video and requesting a type of detection. This request will respond with a name to track the video analysis. Using another request, we periodically check whether processing is complete.

The two requests are:

- The label detection request
- The operation status request

Label detection – request structure

We are going to make a new request as follows:

Field	Value
HTTP method	POST
URL	https://videointelligence.googleapis.com/v1/videos:annotate?key=API_KEY

Request body	```
	// SNIPP SNIPP
	{
	    "inputContent": "/9j/7QBEUGhvdG9zaG9...base64-encoded-video-content...fXNWzvDEeYxxxzj/Coa6Bax//Z",
	    "features": ["LABEL_DETECTION"]
	}
	// SNIPP SNIPP
	``

Note that the `inputContent` property under the image property is the `base64` encoded version of the video. In the same `videos` folder, you should find a file named `Label_Detection-2018228-f88xrq785g_Base64.txt`. This is the `base64` version of the same video. You can use an online service such as `https://www.browserling.com/tools/image to-base64` or `https://www.base64-image.de/` for converting your own video to `base64` string. And, under features, we are requesting the `LABEL_DETECTION` feature.

 Neither Packt Publishing nor the author are endorsing the previous links. Please use them at your own risk.

Label detection – constructing the request

Now, using Postman, we are going to construct a request and fire it to the Google Video Intelligence API. Click on **New** and then **Request** inside Postman. Name the request `label detection`. I have created a new collection named `Video Intelligence API` and placed this request inside that. You can import that collection into your Postman as well. This file is available in the `Chapter 4\API\Postman` folder.

Update the new request as follows:

Field	Value
HTTP method	POST
URL	https://videointelligence.googleapis.com/v1/videos:annotate?key=API_KEY

Request body	```
	// SNIPP SNIPP
	{
	    "inputContent": "/9j/7QBEUGhvdG9zaG9...base64-encoded-video-content...fXNWzvDEeYxxxzj/Coa6Bax//Z",
	
	    "features": ["LABEL_DETECTION"]
	}
	// SNIPP SNIPP
	``

In the previous fields, update the API Key and base64 encoded string, as applicable.

Label detection – analyze response

Now, click on **Send** and we should see something like this in Postman:

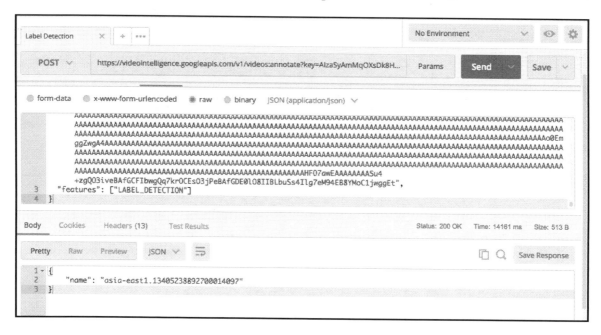

The response consists of a name. Now, using the value of the name property in the response, we will make a request to get the status of the response.

Operation status – request structure

We are going to make a request as follows:

Field	Value
HTTP method	GET
URL	https://videointelligence.googleapis.com/v1/operations/REQUEST_NAME?key=API_KEY

Operation status – constructing the request

Now, using Postman, we are going to construct a request and fire it to the Google Video Intelligence API. Click on **New** and then **Request** inside Postman. Name the request Operation Status. I have created a new collection named Video Intelligence API and placed this request inside that. You can import that collection into your Postman as well. This file is available in the Chapter 4\API\Postman folder. Update the new request as follows:

Field	Value
HTTP method	GET
URL	https://videointelligence.googleapis.com/v1/operations/REQUEST_NAME?key=API_KEY

In the previous fields, update the API key and request name as applicable.

Operation status – analyze response

Now, click on **Send** and we should see something like this in Postman:

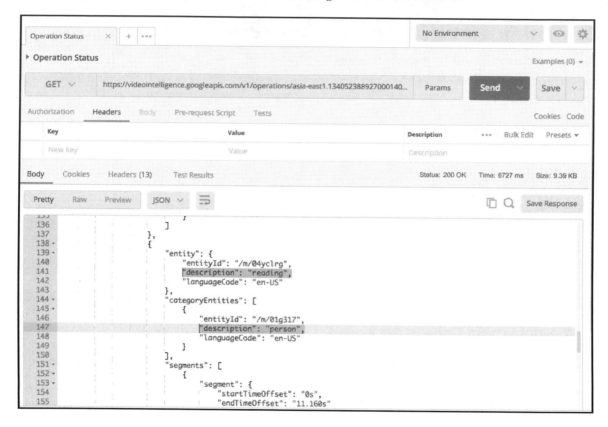

The response we have should look something like this:

```
// SNIPP SNIPP
{
    "name": "asia-east1.13405238892700014097",
    "metadata":
    { ...
    },
    "done": true,
    "response":
    {
        "@type":
"type.googleapis.com/google.cloud.videointelligence.v1.AnnotateVideoRespons
e",
        "annotationResults": [
```

```
            {
        "segmentLabelAnnotations": [
            {
                "entity":
                {
                    "entityId": "...",
                    "description": "...",
                    "languageCode": "..."
                },
                "segments": [
                {
                    "segment":
                    {
                        "startTimeOffset": "...",
                        "endTimeOffset": "..."
                    },
                    "confidence": ...
                }]
            },
            ...
        ],
        "shotLabelAnnotations": [
            {
                "entity":
                {
                    "entityId": "...",
                    "description": "...",
                    "languageCode": "..."
                },
                "segments": [
                {
                    "segment":
                    {
                        "startTimeOffset": "...",
                        "endTimeOffset": "..."
                    },
                    "confidence": ...
                }]
            },
            ...
        ]
    }]
    }
}
// SNIPP SNIPP
```

I have removed a lot of data for brevity. The `name` and `metadata` properties return the request information, `done` indicates whether the request is still in process or if it is completed, and the `response` property consists of the actual response. For label detection, we use `segmentLabelAnnotations` and `shotLabelAnnotations`. `segmentLabelAnnotations` provides us with information on various labels at given time segments, along with confidence. shotLabelAnnotations also provides us with entity information at various segments.

 To analyze a video for a given feature, we make the first request to post the video and kick off the analysis, and we then make another API call to get the status.

This means that we are making two API calls to get the actual response, and not one. Imagine if our operation status request returned done as false (done will be in JSON response if the request is still being processed); we will make another request in, say, 10 seconds. That means we have made three API calls so far and there is no response.

You can view the total API calls made on the Dashboard of the **APIs & Services** service. Now that we have an idea of the API, let's get started with integrating the video intelligence API with *SmartExchange*.

API reference

- You can find the reference for each property in the request object here: `https://cloud.google.com/video-intelligence/docs/reference/rest/v1/videos/annotate#request-body`.
- To get the operation status based on a name returned from Annotate API, refer to `https://cloud.google.com/video-intelligence/docs/reference/rest/v1/operations/get`. A successful response from the `Operation API` will return an `Operation response`.
- You can find more information on operation here: `https://cloud.google.com/video-intelligence/docs/reference/rest/Shared.Types/Operation`.

Integrating Video Intelligence API with SmartExchange

Now that we have seen what can be done using Video Intelligence API, let's actually integrate this into *SmartExchange*. The idea is that we will allow users to record a video and reply to the thread.

Using the Video Intelligence API service, we are going to fetch the video labels as well as check the video for any explicit content using the label detection and explicit content detection features. The final output of the uploaded video and its contents will look as shown here:

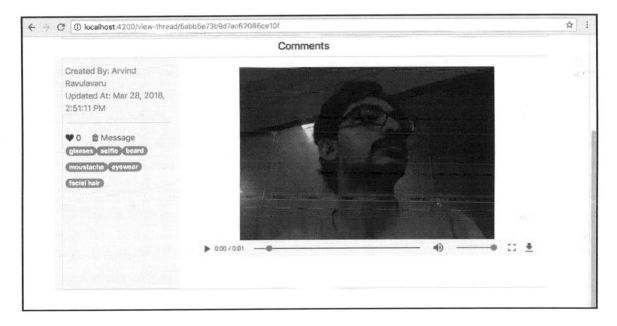

A simple and powerful way to protect the content on our sites, without any administration. So, let's get started with the implementation.

Solution design

To achieve our solution, we are going to do the following:

1. On the view-thread page, we are going to provide a button next to **Reply** named `Reply with Video`, to keep things simple

2. The user is going to record a video using the camera attached to their laptop/computer

3. We are going to the upload that video recording to our server

4. The video will be saved on our servers temporarily

5. The uploaded video will then be sent to Google Video Intelligence API to detect labels and explicit content

6. If the explicit content returns **POSSIBLE** for the `pornographyLikelihood` property on any of the segments in the video, we do not allow the user to upload that video

7. If the video is safe, we then upload it to Cloudinary, as we did in `Chapter 3`, *Cloud Vision API*

8. Once the upload to Cloudinary is successful, we will get back the public URL

9. Using all the data we have gathered so far, we are going to create a new message and then respond with it

10. The Angular app will process the response and update the thread

Uploading videos to Cloudinary is optional. I have implemented it to show an end-to-end flow.

Before we start the implementation, make sure you have the API key for Cloudinary. If not, please refer to *Setting up Cloudinary* section in `Chapter 3`, *Cloud Vision API*, .

Get a copy of code from Chapter 3

Since this is a project based book, the code continues from one chapter to the next. To start working on this chapter's code, please work with your copy of the completed `Chapter 3`, *Cloud Vision API* code. Or, you can get it from `https://github.com/PacktPublishing/Getting-Started-with-Google-Cloud-AI-Services/tree/master/Chapter%204`. Once you have downloaded the code locally from GitHub, make sure you have updated the required API keys and database connections to continue.

Setting up server code

To get started, make sure you are working on the latest code or get a copy from `https://github.com/PacktPublishing/Getting-Started-with-Google-Cloud-AI-Services` and then install the required dependencies by running:

```
$ npm install
or
$ yarn install
```

Now that we have our code base ready, we will continue. Open your `.env` file placed at the root of the *SmartExchange* code, and add the `GCP Service Key` that we created earlier, as shown here:

```
// SNIPP SNIPP
GCP_SK_CREDENTIALS={"type": "service_account", "project_id": "smart-
exchange-b10882", "private_key_id":
"29e9aed0a8aa92c9cc9fcdfa3bd28f7999108c69", "private_key": "-----BEGIN
PRIVATE KEY-----
nMIIEvQIBADANBgkqhkiG9w0BAQEFAASCBKcwggSjAgEAAoIBAQCvedVDQQFIM/Q3n1a9LcurR1
eC9QBGGZzpijB0mHlLhkCZ7V4T16VwkQyoVs3dn67eK/ov4+i4AzW9inOqC8qbt2jJtXYoPiq+0
RP7B+kF8RGNSF41xilvha7dekXAOk7yd11Y8j141DAi1Cn/lwIDDVPWjXzXHeNtP+0J0aJ+wASO
qDeVHbbPdQnneHB76jJZjSO88oHOlQ1UK8HnDR08YImyaLLAGYv0g4qkZYzgIwRBXE13IctS+fD
7JtQrHImn9sxSKqrUp0VZx0RDn4+4LrYWo4BYOWTcgSQjNuzmjPWeAol8DeS5roYlJaggOi7gwJ
a7SBcTbUFV9Hqz2nokJryj2PAgMBAAECggEAG13n6cZAme8oXnDgFudEQheWJk3QreJ5k5cAkMp
X6L/fnkIr0vJl5elpTPPExZS65AF90mw8Bj7R6c5prKSFbkECblYRSx05C+dayAvsnKHZzn5rGv
3axnvv6siACBvP5jLA44NcIIrUC0MvA8JoWPoCJMsKNk5+ArLemBInwk/WJgOnCKiwamDtUV3EJQ
td69CJXGqo07jDODaoXaStsseWhK+vbKN9IeU0msupuW9qIlxznXlSMc2iuk3FSQGGqSqfTK0Wx
Jawhu4d59ftYKujhvlPN6rqcAOEQg/BcRVOm+S5vn93pX2tJvJhC5yqSTiecSfQL9ndjye55tun
DfGSUnUQKBgQDb71zxruFngzmtD4FTn81/1OhnoiS4tZ1MU8P1jn9etBqj58OKTst07z8aylcPE
u+SbX0Kg/xLneGfK2wQcn7D+ZPOI11U7BTasmUcNSxGWGN3fnPY4QNROQisTxeyKfG8ptj5q73n
Fj35YX0a6/nip/akejOx7SWEdX3ImQL888BmQKBgQDMQB/X2ZlR6QRD2tfaYRijttUXQfI63hLT
nqRVG3LJOcz0tSt8P90DOnhzZNgfllciAm14oDLEpnf/W2gdGrfy7olK9mRldDvW7nxvbzVeHRI
IfUi150h7KRKF2kthHoqC8FEO13jnTfvYlNs7MQYO4jS4W3A31IbyS1ntQUktdcBZwKBgEXWCcN
MbpJ53rSPOde4bfjRrCxkct9D8eOyaiNaPBfbB4jl7mxLn3WgCn+tRFuq/ZuXXJ8cLd6s8VmjZh
sLQWZmE9ad2Zh2HVhNC3yzG5B3sOwyYRSXsnVJwPFF5BZUr0fiCv+sgw5/x4oKZLlJuJnxy+PBh
83WDRpQlmSDJrZo3xAoGBAKh0nHo8kTPosRzM7c5kNSYgEi5zB6+i3LSnaIs0tyfU/v+3x+SSu1
IlUCBDxKfQk45eGnDFLVnOvo/o8RhLy7VFzgFIOAmFWSuAKlpxir9TFIKOyFsi7sZc6oTwtAima
rO90enx+s54oIRDQPDuGRCvUTozaBSRWqPF+SxJkvPmULzAoGADdIjNfkScWwGuOYx7iAynksvW
Y2vLlzh0enFpTWJt6mBRSN5kabWxP3iotwnlf4TmNIsSmRobn581DWs+syiun7fijYqEPhCc4gA
A51sxF61i55CdpbcXQVzxoEReVFChMGkLDBNbdJb+tas84c+pLn6igyeYEObc15xeh8mccXZww=
n-----END PRIVATE KEY-----n", "client_email": "smart-exchange-service-
account@smart-exchange-b10882.iam.gserviceaccount.com", "client_id":
"112231488660260011184", "auth_uri":
"https://accounts.google.com/o/oauth2/auth", "token_uri":
"https://accounts.google.com/o/oauth2/token",
"auth_provider_x509_cert_url":
```

```
"https://www.googleapis.com/oauth2/v1/certs", "client_x509_cert_url":
"https://www.googleapis.com/robot/v1/metadata/x509/smart-exchange-service-a
ccount%40smart-exchange-b10882.iam.gserviceaccount.com"}
```

Earlier in this chapter, we created a service account key, which we downloaded as JSON and set up in our environment variables. To keep thing simple, I am not going to read the service account key from the environment variables of my machine, but we are going to add them explicitly for this project using the .env file. This way, I can have multiple projects on my machine using different Google Project's service account keys.

In the previous snippet, we created a new environment variable named GCP_SK_CREDENTIALS and assigned the JSON as one long string, without any line breaks. To convert a JSON string to a single-line string, you can use an online resource such as http://removelinebreaks.net/. If you copy/paste the service account key as is, the application will crash.

Installing dependencies

We are going to install only one dependency, @google-cloud/video-intelligence (https://www.npmjs.com/package/@google-cloud/video-intelligence). If you recall from earlier, we need to make two HTTP requests to get the video response and, if the processing is not done by the second request, we need to keep polling till this is completed. So, to make this process simple, we are going to use the @google-cloud/video-intelligence npm. Run the following command from the root of the application:

```
$ npm install --save @google-cloud/video-intelligence
```

Or run this:

```
$ yarn add @google-cloud/video-intelligence
```

Defining routes

Now that we have the required dependencies, we will update the routes. To work with the Video Intelligence API feature, we are going to add only one new route, which will accept a file, process it, and respond based on the response from Video Intelligence API. Update server/routes/cloud-ai-api.ts and add the upload-video route, as shown here:

```
// SNIPP SNIPP

// Upload Single Images
  router.post('/upload-image/:threadId', Authenticate, Authorize('user'),
```

```
upload.single('image-reply'), cloudAIAPI.uploadImage);

// Upload Single Video
  router.post('/upload-video/:threadId', Authenticate, Authorize('user'),
upload.single('video-reply'), cloudAIAPI.uploadVideo);

// SNIPP SNIPP
```

Updating the message model

Next, we are going to update our message model. We are going to save the labels, explicit content detection results, and Cloudinary upload details in the message, similar to what we have done with the Cloud Vision API response. Update `server/models/message.ts` as shown here:

```
// SNIPP SNIPP
  safeSearchProps: {
      type: Schema.Types.Mixed
  },
  explicitVideoAnnotation: [{
      type: Schema.Types.Mixed,
      default: []
  }],
  segmentLabelAnnotations: [{
      type: Schema.Types.Mixed,
      default: []
  }]
// SNIPP SNIPP
```

Updating the controller

Now that are done with defining the routes and updating the model, we will work on the logic discussed in the *Solution design* section earlier. We are going to add a new method to `CloudAIAPI` named `uploadVideo`. Open `server/controllers/cloud-ai-api.ts`, and we will first add the required imports and the `VideoIntelligenceServiceClient` configuration. Before the class definition, add the following code:

```
// SNIPP SNIPP
const video = require('@google-cloud/video-intelligence').v1;
  const client = new video.VideoIntelligenceServiceClient({
      credentials: JSON.parse(process.env.GCP_SK_CREDENTIALS)
  });
// SNIPP SNIPP
```

Using the environment variable we have set in the .env file, we are using the GCP_SK_CREDENTIALS value to initialize a new VideoIntelligenceServiceClient. Next, we are going to create a new method named uploadVideo and get started with converting the video file uploaded by the user to a base64 string, like we did for the image upload:

```
// SNIPP SNIPP
uploadVideo = (req, res) => {
    // console.log('req.file', req.file);
    const filePath = req.file.path;
    this.base64_encode(filePath).then((BASE64_CONTENT) => {})
}
// SNIPP SNIPP
```

Inside the base64_encode() callback, we get started with constructing a request to send to the Video Intelligence API:

```
// SNIPP SNIPP
const request = {
    inputContent: BASE64_CONTENT,
    features: ['EXPLICIT_CONTENT_DETECTION', 'LABEL_DETECTION']
};

client
    .annotateVideo(request)
    .then((results) => {
            const operation = results[0];
            return operation.promise();
        }
        .then(results => {
            // CODE BELOW
        }).catch(err => {
            console.error('ERROR:', err);
            return res.status(500).json(err);
        });
// SNIPP SNIPP
```

Using `annotateVideo()` on the instance of `VideoIntelligenceServiceClient`, we make a request submitting the video and the features we want to detect. In the second promise, we will have the actual response to the video analysis. The code present inside this section will be as follows:

```
// SNIPP SNIPP
// Gets annotations for video
const annotations = results[0].annotationResults[0];
const explicitContentResults = annotations.explicitAnnotation;
const segmentLabelAnnotations = annotations.segmentLabelAnnotations;
// console.log(JSON.stringify(annotations, null, 4));
let isExplicit = false;
let explictLabels = [];
if (explicitContentResults) {
    explicitContentResults.frames.forEach((result) => {
        var o: any = {};
        // console.log('result', JSON.stringify(result, null, 4));
        o.timeOffset = result.timeOffset;
        o.pornographyLikelihood = result.pornographyLikelihood;
        explictLabels.push(JSON.parse(JSON.stringify(o)));
        if (result.pornographyLikelihood > 2) isExplicit = true;
    });
}
let segmentLabels = [];
if (segmentLabelAnnotations) {
    segmentLabelAnnotations.forEach((label) => {
        let o: any = {};
        // console.log('label', JSON.stringify(label, null, 4));
        o.entity = label.entity;
        o.categoryEntities = label.categoryEntities;
        o.segments = label.segments; // array
        segmentLabels.push(JSON.parse(JSON.stringify(o)));
    });
}
if (isExplicit) {
    this.deleteFile(filePath);
    return res.status(400).json({
        message: 'Adult Content is not allowed'
    })
}
// Upload our video to cloudinary for external file hosting
// This is optional & you can use any service for the same
cloudinary.v2.uploader.upload(filePath, {
    resource_type: 'video'
}, (error, result) => {
    // console.log('result: ', result);
    // console.log('error', error);
```

```
    if (error) {
        return res.status(400).json({
            message: error.message
        });
    }
    // CLOUDINARY CODE BELOW
});
// SNIPP SNIPP
```

In the previous code, we fetch `annotationResults` and
extract `explicitAnnotation` and `segmentLabelAnnotations`.
From `explicitContentResults`, we extract `timeOffset`
and `pornographyLikelihood`. And then, from `segmentLabelAnnotations`, we extract
`entity`, `categoryEntities`, and `segments`. If any one of the `explicitContentResults`
returns a possibility of `pornographyLikelihood`, we respond with a bad request. Now
that we have a valid video, we will upload it to Cloudinary:

```
// SNIPP SNIPP
let msg: any = {};
msg.thread = req.params.threadId;
msg.createdBy = req.user;
msg.lastUpdatedBy = req.user;
msg.explicitVideoAnnotation = explictLabels;
msg.segmentLabelAnnotations = segmentLabels;
msg.cloudinaryProps = result;

msg.description = `<div align="center" class="embed-responsive embed-
responsive-16by9">
<video loop class="embed-responsive-item" controls>
<source src="${result.secure_url}">
Your browser does not support the video tag.
</video>
</div>`;

let message = new Message(msg);
message.save((err, msg) => {
    if (err) {
        console.log(err);
        return this.respondErrorMessage(res, err);
    }
    res.status(200).json(msg);
});

// Delete the local file so we don't clutter
this.deleteFile(filePath);
// SNIPP SNIPP
```

Once the upload is completed, we will extract the video URL and build a message description that can display the video and save the message to database. This wraps up our controller logic as well as our service side logic. In the next section, we are going work on the client-side logic.

Setting up client code

We will continue from where we left off in Chapter 3, *Cloud Vision API* on the client side as well.

Setting up recordrtc

On the client side, we are going to let the users record a live video and post it as a response. For this, we are going to use WebRTC (https://webrtc.org/) and an awesome helper library named RecordRTC (https://github.com/muaz-khan/RecordRTC) by Muaz Khan (https://github.com/muaz-khan). In the Command Prompt or Terminal pointing at the application root folder, run the following command to install recordrtc as a dependency:

```
$ npm install --save recordrtc
```

Or, run this:

```
$ yarn add recordrtc
```

Since this is not an Angular component, we are not going to bootstrap it. We are going to utilize it as a global variable.

Modifying the view thread component

I wanted to keep the video recording and upload feature simple. So, along with the existing **Reply with Text** and **Reply with Image**, we are going to add another button named Reply with Video. This button will launch a modal and help us with the record and upload process. Open client/app/view-thread/view-thread.component.html and, next to the **Reply with Image** button at the bottom of the page, add the following code:

```
// SNIPP SNIPP
<div class="col text-center">
 <button class="btn btn-success" type="submit"
(click)="uploadVideo(thread)"><i class="fa fa-video-camera"></i> Reply with
Video</button>
```

```
</div>
// SNIPP SNIPP
```

Next, the required logic for `uploadVideo` will be placed in `client/app/view-thread/view-thread.component.ts` and should be as follows:

```
// SNIPP SNIPP
uploadVideo(thread: Thread) {
 const modalRef = this.modal.open(UploadVideoModal, {
 size: 'lg'
 });
 modalRef.componentInstance.threadId = this.thread._id;
 modalRef.componentInstance.updateThread.subscribe((message) => {
 if (!message) return;
 thread.messages.push(message);
 });
}
// SNIPP SNIPP
```

Here, we are using the `NgbModal` instance to open the upload video component, which we are going to create in a moment. Using the `componentInstance` on `modalRef`, we are sending the thread ID to that component as input. We will be creating an output named `updateThread` on the upload video component and subscribing to that event. `updateThread` receives the newly created message to be added to the existing list of messages in the thread. Add the following import to `client/app/view-thread/view-thread.component.ts`:

```
// SNIPP SNIPP
import { UploadVideoModal } from './upload-video-modal/upload-video-modal';
// SNIPP SNIPP
```

Now, we will create the upload video modal component.

Setting up the upload video modal component

Inside the `client/app/view-thread` folder, create another folder named `upload-video-modal` and inside that, create two files named `upload-video-modal.html` and `upload-video-modal.ts`. Update `client/app/view-thread/upload-video-modal/upload-video-modal.html` as shown here:

```
// SNIPP SNIPP
<div class="modal-header">
 <h4 class="modal-title">Reply with Video</h4>
 <button type="button" class="close" aria-label="Close"
```

```
(click)="activeModal.dismiss('x')">
 <span aria-hidden="true">&times;</span>
 </button>
</div>
<div class="modal-body">
 <div class="form-group">
 <div class="text-center">
 <video #video class="video"></video>
 </div>
 <br>
 <button type="button" class="btn btn-success" [disabled]="isRecording ||
isProcessing" (click)="startRecording()">Record</button>
 <button type="button" class="btn btn-warning" [disabled]="!isRecording ||
isProcessing" (click)="stopRecording()">Stop</button>
 <button type="button" class="btn btn-info" (click)="download()"
[disabled]="!hasRecorded || isProcessing">Download</button>
 </div>
 <ngb-alert type="danger" [dismissible]="false" *ngIf="error">
 <strong>Error!</strong> {{error.message || error}}
 </ngb-alert>
</div>
<div class="modal-footer">
 <label *ngIf="isProcessing">This might take a couple of minutes. Please be
patient</label>
 <i *ngIf="isProcessing" class="fa fa-circle-o-notch fa-spin fa-3x"></i>
 <button type="button" class="btn btn-success" [disabled]="isProcessing ||
!hasRecorded" (click)="reply()">Reply</button>
</div>
// SNIPP SNIPP
```

Here, we have the `video` tag, which we are going to use to show the live recording in progress, as well as a video preview. We have three buttons, one to start recording, one to stop recording, and one to download the recorded video. Apart from that, we have the required error messages and loading indicators. For the required logic, we will get started by adding the imports to `client/app/view-thread/upload-video-modal/upload-video-modal.ts`:

```
// SNIPP SNIPP
import { Component, Input, Output, EventEmitter, ViewChild, AfterViewInit }
from '@angular/core';
import { NgbActiveModal } from '@ng-bootstrap/ng-bootstrap';
import { ActivatedRoute } from '@angular/router';
import { VideoAPIService } from '../../services/video.api.service';
import * as RecordRTC from 'recordrtc/RecordRTC.min';
// SNIPP SNIPP
```

We are going to create the missing dependencies in a moment. Next, we are going to define `UploadVideoModalcomponent` as shown here:

```
// SNIPP SNIPP
@Component({
 selector: 'sm-create-asset-modal',
 templateUrl: './upload-video-modal.html'
})
export class UploadVideoModal implements AfterViewInit {
 @Input() threadId; // fetch from view-thread page
 @Output() updateThread = new EventEmitter < any > (); // Update main
thread with new message
 error: string = '';
 isProcessing: boolean = false;
 isRecording: boolean = false;
 hasRecorded: boolean = false;
 private stream: MediaStream;
 private recordRTC: any;
 @ViewChild('video') video;
}
// SNIPP SNIPP
```

The constructor will be as follows:

```
// SNIPP SNIPP
constructor(
 public activeModal: NgbActiveModal,
 public videoAPIService: VideoAPIService,
 private route: ActivatedRoute
) {}
// SNIPP SNIPP
```

After the component has been initialized, we fetch the video element and set the default state as follows:

```
// SNIPP SNIPP
ngAfterViewInit() {
 // set the initial state of the video
 let video: HTMLVideoElement = this.video.nativeElement;
 video.muted = false;
 video.controls = true;
 video.autoplay = false;
}
// SNIPP SNIPP
```

Now, we will implement the logic to start recording, as shown here:

```
// SNIPP SNIPP
startRecording() {
 this.isRecording = true;
 const video: MediaTrackConstraints = {
 width: 640,
 height: 480
 };
 const mediaConstraints: MediaStreamConstraints = {
 video: video,
 audio: true
 };
 navigator
 .mediaDevices
 .getUserMedia(mediaConstraints)
 .then(this.successCallback.bind(this), this.errorCallback.bind(this));
 // allow users to record maximum of 10 second videos
 setTimeout(() => {
 this.stopRecording();
 }, 10000)
}
// SNIPP SNIPP
```

As we can see from this, we are using `navigator.mediaDevices.getUserMedia()` to start the recording. Once we do that, we will be asked to give permissions to record audio and video. Then, the success callback or error callback are called appropriately. To make the learning process simple and quick, I am allowing users to record a maximum 10 seconds of video. This way, uploads are faster and Cloud Intelligence API responds quickly for us to see results in near-real time. Next, we are going to set up the success and error callbacks:

```
// SNIPP SNIPP
successCallback(stream: MediaStream) {
 let options = {
 mimeType: 'video/webm',
 audioBitsPerSecond: 512000, // 512kbps
 videoBitsPerSecond: 512000 // 512kbps
 };
 this.stream = stream;
 this.recordRTC = RecordRTC(stream, options);
 this.recordRTC.startRecording();
 let video: HTMLVideoElement = this.video.nativeElement;
 video.src = window.URL.createObjectURL(stream);
 this.toggleControls();
}
// SNIPP SNIPP
```

Here, using the RecordRTC API, we kick off the recording and then stream the recording in the video tag. And, here is the errorCallback():

```
// SNIPP SNIPP
errorCallback() {
 console.error('Somethig went horribly wrong!!', this);
}
// SNIPP SNIPP
```

Now, we will set up stopRecording() as shown here:

```
// SNIPP SNIPP
stopRecording() {
 let recordRTC = this.recordRTC;
 recordRTC.stopRecording(this.processVideo.bind(this));
 let stream = this.stream;
 stream.getAudioTracks().forEach(track => track.stop());
 stream.getVideoTracks().forEach(track => track.stop());
 this.hasRecorded = true;
 this.isRecording = false;
}
// SNIPP SNIPP
```

Using the recordRTC.stopRecording API, we stop the recording and pass in a callback named processVideo to process the video after the recording has stopped. processVideo will be as follows:

```
// SNIPP SNIPP
processVideo(audioVideoWebMURL) {
 let video: HTMLVideoElement = this.video.nativeElement;
 video.src = audioVideoWebMURL;
 this.toggleControls();
}
// SNIPP SNIPP
```

Here, we read the data URL of the stream and then set it to the video element for a preview. For the user to download the video, we will have the following method:

```
// SNIPP SNIPP
download() {
 this.recordRTC.save(this.genFileName());
}
// SNIPP SNIPP
```

We have a couple of helper functions, shown here:

```
// SNIPP SNIPP
genFileName() {
 return 'video_' + (+new Date()) + '_.webm';
}

toggleControls() {
 let video: HTMLVideoElement = this.video.nativeElement;
 video.muted = !video.muted;
 video.controls = !video.controls;
 video.autoplay = !video.autoplay;
}
// SNIPP SNIPP
```

Once the recording is done and the user is ready to reply with that video, we will use `reply()` as shown here:

```
// SNIPP SNIPP
reply() {
 this.error = '';
 this.isProcessing = true;
 let recordedBlob = this.recordRTC.getBlob();
 recordedBlob.name = this.genFileName();
 this.videoAPIService.postFile(this.threadId, recordedBlob).subscribe(data
=> {
 console.log(data);
 this.updateThread.emit(data);
 this.isProcessing = false;
 this.activeModal.close();
 }, error => {
 console.log(error);
 this.error = error.error;
 this.isProcessing = false;
 });
}
// SNIPP SNIPP
```

This concludes our upload video modal component. Before we proceed, we need to add this component to `client/app/app.module.ts`. First, let's import `UploadVideoModal` into `client/app/app.module.ts`:

```
// SNIPP SNIPP
import { UploadVideoModal } from './view-thread/upload-video-modal/upload-
video-modal';
// SNIPP SNIPP
```

Next, we will add this modal to `declarations` as well as `entryComponents`, as shown here:

```
// SNIPP
declarations: [
    AppComponent,
    AboutComponent,
    RegisterComponent,
    LoginComponent,
    LogoutComponent,
    AccountComponent,
    AdminComponent,
    NotFoundComponent,
    HomeComponent,
    CreateThreadComponent,
    ViewThreadComponent,
    FilterThreadPipe,
    EditThreadComponent,
    UploadImageModal,
    UploadVideoModal
],
entryComponents: [
    UploadImageModal,
    UploadVideoModal
],
// SNIPP
```

Save all the files and we are good to move on.

Completing the view thread component

Now that we have the upload video component done, we will complete minor UI changes to the view thread page, which will present the data we have gathered in a better way. Open `client/app/view-thread/view thread.component.html` and update the card, which displays the message with the `segmentLabelAnnotations` data, as shown here:

```
<label class="badge badge-pill badge-info" *ngFor="let s of
message.segmentLabelAnnotations">
    {{s.entity.description}}
</label>
```

Add this after the `message.labels` content that we created to display image labels. To complete the component, we will update the `sanitizeContent` helper in `client/app/view-thread/view-thread.component.ts` as shown here:

```
sanitizeContent(content: string) {
    if (content.indexOf('<video') > 0) return content;
    return this.sanitizer.bypassSecurityTrustHtml(content);
}
```

Save all the files and move on.

Creating the video API service

To upload the image to our server, we are using `postFile()` on `videoAPIService`. Let's create this service now. Inside the `client/app/services` folder, create a file named `video.api.service.ts` and update it, as shown here:

```
import { Injectable } from '@angular/core';
import { HttpClient } from '@angular/common/http';
import { Observable } from 'rxjs/Observable';

@Injectable()
export class VideoAPIService {
    constructor(private http: HttpClient) {}
    postFile(threadId: string, videoBlob: File): Observable < any > {
        const formData: FormData = new FormData(),
        formData.append('video-reply', videoBlob, videoBlob.name);
        return this.http.post < any > (`/api/upload-video/${threadId}`,
formData);
    }
}
```

Finally, we need to add this service as a provider in `client/app/app.module.ts`. First, we will import `VideoAPIService` into `client/app/app.module.ts`:

```
import { VideoAPIService } from './services/video.api.service';
```

And update, `providers` as shown here:

```
// SNIPP SNIPP
providers: [
    AuthService,
    AuthGuardLogin,
    AuthGuardAdmin,
    UserService,
```

```
        ThreadService,
        MessageService,
        VisionAPIService,
        VideoAPIService,
        {
            provide: HTTP_INTERCEPTORS,
            useClass: TokenInterceptor,
            multi: true
        }
    ],
    // SNIPP SNIPP
```

Save all the files and continue.

Testing the app

To test the app, from the root of the application folder, run:

```
$ npm run dev
```

Or, run this:

```
$ yarn dev
```

This will launch our application. From the home page, click on **Create Thread** and create a new thread named Video API Test, or any name you like. Once we create a new thread, and navigate to the view thread page, we should see the new reply section, as shown here:

When we click on **Reply with Video**, we should see a popup where you can record a video and then preview it and download it. Once we click on the **record** button, we should see the browser asking the user permissions to capture audio and video:

Once permission has been given, the recording begins:

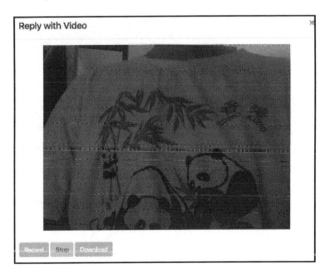

Now, when we click on **Reply**, the video will get uploaded to our server first, and then it will upload the same video to Video Intelligence API to get the Explicit Content Annotations and Segment Label Annotations. If everything is as expected, this video is uploaded to Cloudinary, a public URL of this video is fetched, and the description for this video is constructed and sent back. This is how the final message will look:

The labels appear on the left side of the message. You can try recording various videos and test the complete flow end to end.

Keep an eye on the number of API requests you are making to Video Intelligence API as well as Cloudinary.

To wrap up this chapter, we are going to push the code to Heroku.

Deploying to Heroku

This step is optional, and you can do it if you are interested in deploying this app to Heroku. To continue with this section, you need to have set up a Heroku account and installed the Heroku Toolbelt. Once that is done, open a new Command Prompt or Terminal inside the `smart-exchange-base` folder, then run:

```
$ heroku login
```

This is a prompt for the Heroku credentials that you have signed up with. Next, let's get our application ready for deployment. Run this:

```
$ npm run build
```

Or, run this:

```
$ yarn build
```

This will run the required scripts to build the final `dist` folder, which will be deployed to Heroku. Once the build is completed, run the following:

```
$ git add -A
$ git commit -am "Video Intelligence API Integration Commit"
```

Let's push the code to Heroku. Run this:

```
$ git push heroku master
```

If everything goes well, the code will be uploaded to Heroku and you should be able to view the application at `https://smart-exchange.herokuapp.com`.

Summary

In this chapter, we went through the Google Video Intelligence API and we worked with two features of the API. Then, we set up the required code to integrate this API with the *SmartExchange* app. In the next chapter, we are going to work with the Cloud Speech API.

Cloud Speech API

5

In the last chapter, we saw how to work with Video Intelligence API and how we can integrate the Video Intelligence API with *SmartExchange* to detect the labels in video, as well as detect explicit content. In this chapter, we are going to work with Cloud Speech API. We are going to let users reply with an audio recording from the browser using WebRTC. We are then going to send this audio sample to Cloud Speech API to get its content in English. This way, we can get the text from the audio to perform a search, or detect the sentiment of the content later on.

The topics covered are:

- What is Video Intelligence API?
- Exploring Video Intelligence API
- Integrating Video Intelligence API with *SmartExchange*

Cloud Speech API

Google Cloud Speech API is one of the machine learning services exposed under the Cloud AI vertical. This service is used to detect the contents/text of audio using neural networks.

This service can:

- Work in noisy environments
- Perform context-aware recognition
- Support streaming results
- Support conversion in over 110 languages
- Support global vocabulary
- Perform inappropriate content filtering

Pricing

The pricing for this service is as follows:

Usage	Price
0-60 mins	Free
61-1 million mins	$0.006 for every 15 secs

You can read more about pricing here: `https://cloud.google.com/speech/#cloud-speech-api-pricing`.

Now that we have the basics of the Vision API and understand the pricing model, let's get started with hands-on exploration. Before we get started, we need to set up the required authentication and authorization. In the next section, we are going to look at that.

 When working with any Google Cloud AI service, we need to have either an API key or a service account key set up. Before we set up the API key or a service account, we need to have a Google Cloud project. If you already have a project, you can skip that section. Please refer to *Setting up an authentication* section from `Chapter 2`, *Setting Up a Smart Forum App*.

Enabling the API

Now that we have a project and we have both API and Service Account Keys, we will enable the required API and test our application. Navigate to the project home page (`https://console.cloud.google.com/home/dashboard?project=smart-exchange-b10882`). From the menu on the left-hand side, select **APIs & Services | Library**. Once we land on this page, search for *Cloud Speech API* and click on that card. Then, click on the **Enable** button. This will prompt you to set up billing, if you have not already done this. Once you have enabled billing and the API, you should see that the **Cloud Speech API** is enabled:

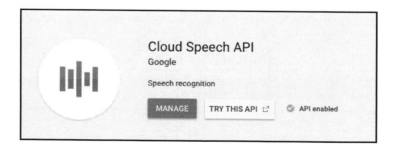

In the next section, we are going to explore the API.

Exploring the Cloud Speech API

Please refer to the *Setting up a rest client* section from `Chapter 3`, *Cloud Vision API*, to set up a REST API client, either Postman or cURL, before you continue. Now that we have all the required setup done, let's get started with exploring the API. In this section, we are going to upload a single channel, *Linear16* encoded, with a 44100 sample rate, in `base64` format, to Cloud Speech API and get its transcription. There are three ways we can convert audio to text using the Cloud Speech API:

- Synchronous speech recognition
- Asynchronous speech recognition
- Streaming speech recognition

Synchronous speech recognition

If our audio file is less than 1 minute, Synchronous speech recognition is a good fit. The results of the request are near real-time, that is, the transcription results are sent along with the response to this request. We are going to use Synchronous speech Recognition in our application and exploration.

Asynchronous speech recognition

If our audio file is longer than a minute and is available on Google Cloud Storage, we can use this service to convert audio to text.

Streaming speech recognition

Streaming speech recognition allows us to stream an audio to the Cloud Speech API and receive speech streaming in real-time as the audio is processed. While working with any of the previous three approaches, keep an eye on audio limits: `https://cloud.google.com/speech/quotas`.

Audio to text using synchronous speech recognition

In the project folder that you downloaded along with this book, or at `https://github.com/PacktPublishing/Getting-Started-with-Google-Cloud-AI-Services`, you can find a folder for `Chapter 5`, and inside that folder you will find another folder named `API`, and inside that folder a folder named `Audio`. Inside the `Audio` folder, I placed the `sample audio` file that I used for testing, for your reference. You are free to use any audio sample, as long as it is a single-channel audio with the encoding defined here: `https://cloud.google.com/speech/reference/rest/v1/RecognitionConfig#AudioEncoding`. From inside the `API \ Audio` folder, refer to `audio arvind_sample_recording.wav`. The content of the audio file are me enunciating *this is a sample recording*.

Request structure

We are going to make a request as follows:

Field	Value
HTTP method	POST
URL	`https://speech.googleapis.com/v1/speech:recognize?key=API_KEY`

Request body	`// SNIPP SNIPP`
	`{`
	`  "config":`
	`  {`
	`  "encoding": "LINEAR16",`
	`  "sampleRateHertz": 44100,`
	`  "languageCode": "en-us"`
	`  },`
	`  "audio":`
	`  {`
	`  "content": "-- BASE64 AUDIO CONTTENT --"`
	`  }`
	`}`
	`// SNIPP SNIPP`

Note that the content property under the audio property is the base64 encoded version of the audio. In the same Audio folder, you should find a file named arvind_sample_recording_base64.txt. This is the base64 version of the same audio. You can use an online service such as https://www.browserling.com/tools/image-to-base64 or https://www.base64-image.de/ for converting your own audio to a base64 string.

Neither Packt Publishing nor the author are endorsing the previous links. Please use them at your own risk.

Constructing the request

Now, using Postman, we are going to construct a request and fire it to the Google Speech API. Click on **New** and then **Request** inside Postman, and provide a name as applicable. I created a new collection named Cloud Speech API and placed this request inside that. You can import that collection into your Postman as well. This file is available in the Chapter 5\API\Postman folder. Update the new request as follows:

Field	Value
HTTP method	POST
URL	https://speech.googleapis.com/v1/speech:recognize?key=API_KEY

Request body	```
	// SNIPP SNIPP
	{
	  "config":
	  {
	  "encoding": "LINEAR16",
	  "sampleRateHertz": 44100,
	  "languageCode": "en-us"
	  },
	  "audio":
	  {
	  "content": "-- BASE64 AUDIO CONTTENT --"
	  }
	}
	// SNIPP SNIPP
	``

In the previous fields, update the API key and base64 encoded string as applicable.

Analyse response

Now, click on **Send** and we should see something like this in Postman:

As we can from the previous results, we got the text from the audio with a confidence of 98%. There are other ways of detecting, as we have seen earlier. You can explore more about them here: `https://cloud.google.com/speech/docs/how-to`.

API reference

- You can find the reference for each property in the request object here: `https://cloud.google.com/speech/reference/rest/v1/speech/recognize#request-body`.

- The response object's information is here: `https://cloud.google.com/speech/reference/rest/v1/speech/recognize#response-body`.

Integrating Cloud Speech API with SmartExchange

Now that we have seen what can be done using Cloud Speech API, let's actually integrate this into *SmartExchange*. We will allow the users to post an audio response to a thread by recoding using WebRTC. This audio sample will then be sent to the Cloud Speech API to get the text. In this chapter, we are going to only print the text and let the users view/hear the audio sample. This example can be further extended, which I will talk about in `Chapter 6`, *Cloud Natural Language* . The final output of the uploaded audio and its contents will look as shown here:

So, let's get started with the implementation.

Solution design

To achieve our solution, we are going to do the following:

1. On the view-thread page, we are going to provide a button next to **Reply** named `Reply with Audio` to keep things simple

2. The user is going to record an audio to our server using this interface
3. The audio will be saved on our servers temporarily
4. The uploaded audio will then be sent to Cloud Speech API to detect text
5. Once we get back the response, we upload this to Cloudinary, a file hosting service
6. Once the upload to Cloudinary is successful, we will get back the public URL
7. Using all the data we have gathered so far, we are going to create a new message and then respond with it
8. The Angular app will process the response and update the thread

 Uploading audio to Cloudinary is optional. I implemented it to show an end-to-end flow.

Before we start the implementation, please make sure you have an API key for Cloudinary.

Setting up the server code

To get started, make sure you are working on the latest code or get a copy from `https://github.com/PacktPublishing/Getting-Started-with-Google-Cloud-AI-Services` and then install the required dependencies by running:

```
$ npm install
or
$ yarn install
```

In the last chapter, we already added `GCP_SK_CREDENTIALS` to our `.env` file. Make sure this is present and is accurate for us to continue.

Installing dependencies

We are going to install only one dependency, @google-cloud/speech (https://www.
npmjs.com/package/@google-cloud/speech), to interface with the Cloud Speech API. Run
this command from the root of the application:

```
$ npm install --save @google-cloud/speech
or
$ yarn add @google-cloud/speech
```

Defining routes

Now that we have the required dependencies, we will update the routes. To work with
Cloud Speech API, we are going to add only one route that will accept a file, process it, and
respond based on the response from Cloud Speech API. Update server/routes/cloud-
ai-api.ts and add the upload-audio route, as shown here:

```
// SNIPP SNIPP
router.post('/upload-image/:threadId', Authenticate, Authorize('user'),
upload.single('image-reply'), cloudAIAPI.uploadImage);
router.post('/upload-video/:threadId', Authenticate, Authorize('user'),
upload.single('video-reply'), cloudAIAPI.uploadVideo);
router.post('/upload-audio/:threadId', Authenticate, Authorize('user'),
upload.single('audio-reply'), cloudAIAPI.uploadAudio);
// SNIPP SNIPP
```

Updating the message model

Next, we are going to update our message model. We are going to save the transcription
results and Cloudinary upload details as well in the message, similar to what we did with
the Cloud Vision API response. Update server/models/message.ts as shown here:

```
// SNIPP SNIPP
explicitVideoAnnotation: [{
        type: Schema.Types.Mixed,
        default: []
    }],
    segmentLabelAnnotations: [{
        type: Schema.Types.Mixed,
        default: []
    }],
    transcriptions: [{
        type: Schema.Types.Mixed,
        default: []
```

```
    }]
// SNIPP SNIPP
```

Updating the controller

Now that are done with defining the routes and updating the model, we will work on the logic as discussed in the *Solution design* section earlier. We are going to add a new method to `CloudAIAPI` named `uploadAudio`. Open `server/controllers/cloud-ai-api.ts` and we will first add the required imports, and `SpeechClientconfiguration`. Before the class definition, add this code:

```
// SNIPP SNIPP
const speech = require('@google-cloud/speech');
const speechClient = new speech.SpeechClient({
    credentials: JSON.parse(process.env.GCP_SK_CREDENTIALS)
});
// SNIPP SNIPP
```

Using the environment variable we set in the `.env` file, we are using the `GCP_SK_CREDENTIALS` value to initialize a new `SpeechClient`. Next, we are going to create a new method named `uploadAudio` and get started with converting the audio file uploaded by the user to a `base64` string, like we did for the image upload:

```
// SNIPP SNIPP
uploadAudio = (req, res) => {
    // console.log('req.file', req.file);
    const filePath = req.file.path;
    this.base64_encode(filePath).then((BASE64_CONTENT) => {})
}
// SNIPP SNIPP
```

Inside the `base64_encode()` callback, we get started with constructing a request to send to the Cloud Speech API:

```
// SNIPP SNIPP
const config = {
    encoding: 'LINEAR16',
    sampleRateHertz: 44100,
    languageCode: 'en-us',
};
const audio = {
    content: BASE64_CONTENT
};
const request = {
    config: config,
```

```
        audio: audio,
};
speechClient
    .recognize(request)
    .then((data) => {
        // CODE BELOW
    })
    .catch(err => {
        console.error('ERROR:', err);
        return res.status(500).json(err);
    });
// SNIPP SNIPP
```

Using `recognize ()` on the instance of `SpeechClient`, we make a request submitting the `audio` and the `config`. The code present inside this section will be as follows:

```
// SNIPP SNIPP
const transcriptions = [];
const response = data[0];
response.results.forEach((result) => {
    let o: any = {};
    o.transcript = result.alternatives[0].transcript;
    o.words = result.alternatives[0].words;
    o.confidence = result.alternatives[0].confidence;
    transcriptions.push(o);
});
cloudinary.v2.uploader.upload(filePath, {
    resource_type: 'auto'
}, (error, result) => {
    //CODE BELOW
});
// SNIPP SNIPP
```

In the previous code, we extracted the results from the response and, using `forEach`, we processed `alternatives[0]` and stored the `transcript`, `words`, and `confidence`. Now that we have the text for the audio, we will upload it to Cloudinary:

```
// SNIPP SNIPP
if (error) {
    return res.status(400).json({
        message: error.message
    });
}
let msg: any = {};
msg.thread = req.params.threadId;
msg.createdBy = req.user;
msg.lastUpdatedBy = req.user;
```

```
msg.transcriptions = transcriptions;
msg.cloudinaryProps = result;
msg.description = `<div align="center" class="embed-responsive-16by9">
<audio class="embed-responsive-item" controls>
<source src="${result.secure_url}">
Your browser does not support the audio tag.
</audio>
</div>`
let message = new Message(msg);
message.save((err, msg) => {
    if (err) {
        console.log(err);
        return this.respondErrorMessage(res, err);
    }
    res.status(200).json(msg);
});
// Delete the local file so we don't clutter
this.deleteFile(filePath);
// SNIPP SNIPP
```

Once the upload is completed, we will extract the audio URL, and build a message description that can display the HTML5 audio player and then save the message to the database. This wraps up our controller logic and our service side logic. In the next section, we are going work on the client-side logic.

Setting up the client code

We will continue from where we left off in Chapter 4, *Video Intelligence API*. Since we already set up all the needed dependencies in the last chapter, we will continue with the development.

Modifying the view thread component

I wanted to keep the audio record and upload feature simple. So, along with the existing reply with text, reply with image, and reply with video features, we are going to add another button named **Reply with Audio**; this button will launch a modal and help us with the record and upload process. Open client/app/view-thread/view-thread.component.html and, next to the **Reply with Video** button at the bottom of the page, add this code:

```
// SNIPP SNIPP
<div class="col text-center">
 <button class="btn btn-dark" type="submit"
```

```
(click)="uploadAudio(thread)"><i class="fa fa-microphone"></i> Reply with
Audio</button>
</div>
// SNIPP SNIPP
```

Next, the required logic for `uploadAudio` will be placed in `client/app/view-thread/view-thread.component.ts` and should be this:

```
// SNIPP SNIPP
uploadAudio(thread: Thread) {
 const modalRef - this.modal.open(UploadAudioModal, {
 size: 'lg'
 });
 modalRef.componentInstance.threadId = this.thread._id;
 modalRef.componentInstance.updateThread.subscribe((message) => {
 if (!message) return;
 thread.messages.push(message);
 });
}
// SNIPP SNIPP
```

Here, we are using the `NgbModal` instance to open the upload audio component, which we are going to create in a moment. Using the `componentInstance` on `modalRef`, we are sending in the thread ID to that component as input. We will be creating an output named `updateThread` on the Upload Audio component and subscribing to that event. `updateThread` sends back the newly created message to be added to the existing list of messages in the thread. Add this import to `client/app/view-thread/view-thread.component.ts`:

```
// SNIPP SNIPP
import { UploadAudioModal } from './upload-audio-modal/upload-audio-modal';
// SNIPP SNIPP
```

Now, we will create the upload video audio component.

Setting up the upload audio modal component

Inside the `client/app/view-thread` folder, create another folder named `upload-audio-modal` and inside that, create two files named `upload-audio-modal.html` and `upload-audio-modal.ts`. Update `client/app/view-thread/upload-audio-modal/upload-audio-modal.html` as shown here:

```
// SNIPP SNIPP
<div class="modal-header">
```

```
  <h4 class="modal-title">Reply with Audio</h4>
  <button type="button" class="close" aria-label="Close"
(click)="activeModal.dismiss('x')">
  <span aria-hidden="true">&times;</span>
  </button>
</div>
<div class="modal-body">
 <div class="form-group">
 <div class="text-center">
 <audio #audio class="audio" controls></audio>
 </div>
 <br>
 <button type="button" class="btn btn-success" [disabled]="isRecording ||
isProcessing" (click)="startRecording()">Record</button>
 <button type="button" class="btn btn-warning" [disabled]="!isRecording ||
isProcessing" (click)="stopRecording()">Stop</button>
 <button type="button" class="btn btn-info" (click)="download()"
[disabled]="!hasRecorded || isProcessing">Download</button>
 </div>
 <ngb-alert type="danger" [dismissible]="false" *ngIf="error">
 <strong>Error!</strong> {{error.details || error.message || error}}
 </ngb-alert>
</div>
<div class="modal-footer">
 <label *ngIf="isProcessing">This might take a couple of minutes. Please be
patient</label>
 <i *ngIf="isProcessing" class="fa fa-circle-o-notch fa-spin fa-3x"></i>
 <button type="button" class="btn btn-success" [disabled]="isProcessing ||
!hasRecorded" (click)="reply()">Reply</button> </div>
// SNIPP SNIPP
```

Here, we have an audio tag, which we are going to use to show the audio preview. We have three buttons, one to start recording, one to stop recording, and one to download the recorded audio. Apart from that, we have the required error messages and loading indicators. For the required logic, we will get started by adding the imports to client/app/view-thread/upload-audio-modal/upload-audio-modal.ts:

```
// SNIPP SNIPP
import { Component, Input, Output, EventEmitter, ViewChild, AfterViewInit }
from '@angular/core';
import { NgbActiveModal } from '@ng-bootstrap/ng-bootstrap';
import { ActivatedRoute } from '@angular/router';
import { AudioAPIService } from '../../services/audio.api.service';
import * as RecordRTC from 'recordrtc/RecordRTC.min';
// SNIPP SNIPP
```

We are going to create the missing dependencies in a moment. Next, we are going to define the `UploadAudioModal` component as shown here:

```
// SNIPP SNIPP
@Component({
  selector: 'sm-create-asset-modal',
  templateUrl: './upload-audio-modal.html'
})
export class UploadAudioModal implements AfterViewInit {
  @Input() threadId; // fetch from view-thread page
  @Output() updateThread = new EventEmitter < any > (); // Update main
thread with new message
  error: string = '';
  isProcessing: boolean = false;
  isRecording: boolean = false;
  hasRecorded: boolean = false;
  private stream: MediaStream;
  private recordRTC: any;
  @ViewChild('audio') audio;
}
// SNIPP SNIPP
```

The constructor will be as follows:

```
// SNIPP SNIPP
constructor(
  public activeModal: NgbActiveModal,
  public audioAPIService: AudioAPIService,
  private route: ActivatedRoute
) {}
// SNIPP SNIPP
```

After the component has been initialized, we fetch the audio element and set the default state as follows:

```
// SNIPP SNIPP
ngAfterViewInit() {
  // set the initial state of the video
  let audio: HTMLAudioElement = this.audio.nativeElement;
  audio.muted = false;
  audio.controls = true;
  audio.autoplay = false;
  audio.preload = 'auto';
}
// SNIPP SNIPP
```

Now, we will implement the logic to start recording, as shown here:

```
// SNIPP SNIPP
startRecording() {
 this.isRecording = true;
 const mediaConstraints: MediaStreamConstraints = {
 video: false, // Only audio recording
 audio: true
 };
 navigator
 .mediaDevices
 .getUserMedia(mediaConstraints)
 .then(this.successCallback.bind(this), this.errorCallback.bind(this));
 // allow users to record maximum of 10 second audios
 setTimeout(() => {

 this.stopRecording();
 }, 10000)
}
// SNIPP SNIPP
```

As we can see, we are using the navigator called `.mediaDevices.getUserMedia()` to start the recording. Once we do that, we will be asked to give permissions to record audio, if not done already. Then, the `successcallback` or `errorcallback` is called appropriately. To make the learning process simple and quick, I am allowing users to record a maximum 10 seconds of audio. This way, uploads are faster and Cloud Speech API responds quickly for us to see results in near real-time. Next, we are going to set up the success and error callbacks:

```
// SNIPP SNIPP
successCallback(stream: MediaStream) {
 let options = {
 recorderType: RecordRTC.StereoAudioRecorder,
 mimeType: 'audio/wav',
 // Must be single channel:
https://cloud.google.com/speech/reference/rest/v1/RecognitionConfig#AudioEn
coding
 numberOfAudioChannels: 1
 };
 this.stream = stream;
 this.recordRTC = RecordRTC(stream, options);
 this.recordRTC.startRecording();
 let audio: HTMLAudioElement = this.audio.nativeElement;
 audio.src = window.URL.createObjectURL(stream);
 this.toggleControls();
}
// SNIPP SNIPP
```

Here, using the `RecordRTC` API, we kick off the recording and then stream the recording to the `audio` tag. And, here is `errorCallback()`:

```
// SNIPP SNIPP
errorCallback() {
  console.error('Something went horribly wrong!!', this);
}
// SNIPP SNIPP
```

Now, we will set up `stopRecording()` as shown here:

```
// SNIPP SNIPP
stopRecording() {
  let recordRTC = this.recordRTC;
  recordRTC.stopRecording(this.processAudio.bind(this));
  let stream = this.stream;
  stream.getAudioTracks().forEach(track => track.stop());
  stream.getVideoTracks().forEach(track => track.stop());
  this.hasRecorded = true;
  this.isRecording = false
}
// SNIPP SNIPP
```

Using the `recordRTC.stopRecording` API, we stop the recording and pass in a callback named `processAudio` to process the audio after the recording has stopped. `processAudio` would be as follows:

```
// SNIPP SNIPP
processAudio(audioURL) {
  let audio: HTMLAudioElement = this.audio.nativeElement;
  audio.src = audioURL;
  this.toggleControls();
}
// SNIPP SNIPP
```

Here, we read the data URL of the stream and then set it to the audio element for a preview. For the user to download the audio, we will have the following method:

```
// SNIPP SNIPP
download() {
  this.recordRTC.save(this.genFileName());
}
// SNIPP SNIPP
```

We have a couple of helper functions, shown here:

```
// SNIPP SNIPP
genFileName() {
 return 'audio_' + (+new Date()) + '_.wav';
}

toggleControls() {
 let audio: HTMLAudioElement = this.audio.nativeElement;
 audio.muted = !audio.muted;
 audio.autoplay = !audio.autoplay;
 audio.preload = 'auto';
}
// SNIPP SNIPP
```

Once the recording is done and the user is ready to reply with that audio, we will use reply(), as shown here:

```
// SNIPP SNIPP
reply() {
 this.error = '';
 this.isProcessing = true;
 let recordedBlob = this.recordRTC.getBlob();
 recordedBlob.name = this.genFileName();
 this.audioAPIService.postFile(this.threadId, recordedBlob).subscribe(data
=> {
 console.log(data);
 this.updateThread.emit(data);
 this.isProcessing = false;
 this.activeModal.close();
 }, error => {
 console.log(error);
 this.error = error.error;
 this.isProcessing = false;
 });
}
// SNIPP SNIPP
```

This concludes our upload audio modal component. Before we proceed, we need to add this component to client/app/app.module.ts. First, let's import UploadAudioModal into client/app/app.module.ts:

```
// SNIPP SNIPP
import { UploadAudioModal } from './view-thread/upload-audio-modal/upload-
audio-modal';
// SNIPP SNIPP
```

Next, we will add this modal to the declarations and `entryComponents`, as shown here:

```
// SNIPP SNIPP
declarations: [
        AppComponent,
        AboutComponent,
        RegisterComponent,
        LoginComponent,
        LogoutComponent,
        AccountComponent,
        AdminComponent,
        NotFoundComponent,
        HomeComponent,
        CreateThreadComponent,
        ViewThreadComponent,
        FilterThreadPipe,
        EditThreadComponent,
        UploadImageModal,
        UploadVideoModal,
        UploadAudioModal
    ],
    entryComponents: [
        UploadImageModal,
        UploadVideoModal,
        UploadAudioModal
    ],
// SNIPP SNIPP
```

Save all the files, and we are good to move on.

Completing the view thread component

Now that we have the upload audio component done, we will complete minor UI changes to the view thread page, which will present the data we have gathered in a better way. Open `client/app/view-thread/view-thread.component.html` and update the card, which displays the message with the transcriptions data, as shown here:

```
// SNIPP SNIPP
<div class="table-responsive" *ngIf="message.transcriptions.length > 0">
  <table class="table table-bordered">
  <thead class="thead-dark text-center">
  <tr>
  <th scope="col">Transcript</th>
  <th scope="col">Confidence</th>
  <th scope="col">Words</th>
  </tr>
```

```
  </thead>
  <tbody>
  <tr class="text-center" *ngFor="let t of message.transcriptions">
  <th>
  {{t.transcript}}
  </th>
  <th>
  {{(t.confidence * 100).toFixed(5)}} %
  </th>
  <th>
  {{t.words.join(';') || '--'}}
  </th>
  </tr>
  </tbody>
  </table>
</div>
// SNIPP SNIPP
```

Add this after the `safeSearchProps` table that we created to display the `safeSearchProps` image. To complete the component, we will update the `sanitizeContent` helper in `client/app/view-thread/view-thread.component.ts`, as shown here:

```
// SNIPP SNIPP
sanitizeContent(content: string) {
  if (content.indexOf('<video') > 0) return content;
  if (content.indexOf('<audio') > 0) return content;
  return this.sanitizer.bypassSecurityTrustHtml(content);
}
// SNIPP SNIPP
```

Save all the files to move on.

Creating the audio API service

To upload the audio to our server, we are using `postFile()` on `audioAPIService`. Let's create this service now. Inside the `client/app/services` folder, create a file name `audio.api.service.ts` and update it, as shown here:

```
// SNIPP SNIPP
import { Injectable } from '@angular/core';
import { HttpClient } from '@angular/common/http';
import { Observable } from 'rxjs/Observable';
@Injectable()
export class AudioAPIService {
```

```
constructor(private http: HttpClient) {}
postFile(threadId: string, audioBlob: File): Observable < any > {
const formData: FormData = new FormData();
formData.append('audio-reply', audioBlob, audioBlob.name);
return this.http.post < any > (`/api/upload-audio/${threadId}`, formData);
}
}
// SNIPP SNIPP
```

We need to add this service as a provider in client/app/app.module.ts. First, we will import AudioAPIService into client/app/app.module.ts:

```
// SNIPP SNIPP
import { AudioAPIService } from './services/audio.api.service';
// SNIPP SNIPP
```

Update the providers, as shown here:

```
// SNIPP SNIPP
providers: [
    AuthService,
    AuthGuardLogin,
    AuthGuardAdmin,
    UserService,
    ThreadService,
    MessageService,
    VisionAPIService,
    VideoAPIService,
    AudioAPIService,
    {
        provide: HTTP_INTERCEPTORS,
        useClass: TokenInterceptor,
        multi: true
    }
],
// SNIPP SNIPP
```

Save all the files to continue.

Testing the app

To test the app, from the root of the application folder, run this:

```
$ npm run dev
or
$ yarn dev
```

This will launch our application. From the home page, click on **Create Thread** and create a new thread named `Audio API Test`, or any name you like. Once we create a new thread and navigate to the view thread page, we should see the new reply section, as shown here:

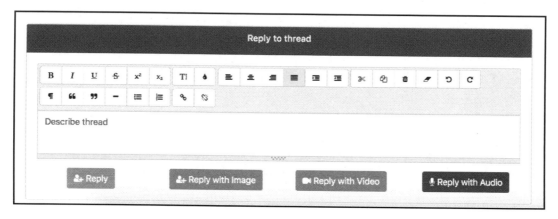

When we click on **Reply with Audio**, we should see a popup where we can record an audio file, and then preview it and download it. Once we click on the **record** button, we should see the browser asking for user permissions to capture audio, if we have not already done so:

Once permission has been given, the recording begins:

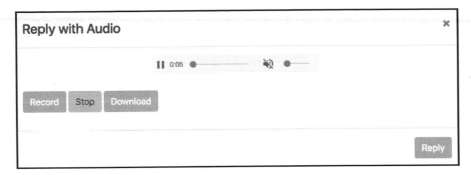

Now, when we click on **Reply**, the audio will get uploaded to our server first, and then our server will upload the same audio to Cloud Speech API to get the transcription. If everything goes as expected, this audio is uploaded to Cloudinary, a public URL of this audio is fetched, and the description for this audio is constructed and sent back. And, this is how the final message will look:

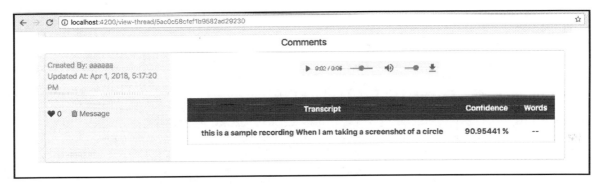

I said *This is a sample recording while I am taking a screenshot of the popup* and this is what Speech API recognized. You can try recording various audio samples and test the complete flow end to end.

 Keep an eye on the number of API requests you are making to the Cloud Speech API and Cloudinary.

To wrap up this chapter, we are going to push the code to Heroku.

Deploying to Heroku

This step is optional, and you can do it if you are interested in deploying this app to Heroku. To continue with this section, you need to set up a Heroku account and install the Heroku tool belt. Once that is done, open a new Command Prompt or Terminal inside the `smart-exchange-base` folder, and then run:

```
$ heroku login
```

This is a prompt for the Heroku credentials that you signed up with. Next, let's get our application ready for deployment. Run this:

```
$ npm run build
```

Or, run this:

```
$ yarn build
```

This will run the required scripts to build the final `dist` folder, which will be deployed to Heroku. Once the build is completed, run the following:

```
$ git add -A
$ git commit -am "Cloud Speech API Integration Commit"
```

Lets push the code to Heroku. Run this:

```
$ git push heroku master
```

If everything goes well, the code will be uploaded to Heroku and you should be able to view the application at `https://smart-exchange.herokuapp.com`.

Summary

In this chapter, we went through the Google Cloud Speech API and we worked with the recognize API. Then, we set up the required code to integrate this API with the *SmartExchange* app.

In the next chapter, we are going to work with the Cloud Natural Language API.

6
Cloud Natural Language

In the last chapter, we learned how to work with Cloud Speech API, and saw how we can integrate the Cloud Speech API with *SmartExchange* to convert speech to text. In this chapter, we are going to work with the Cloud Natural Language API. We are going to let the users reply to a thread using a text message, a function we already have now. Before we save that message to the database, we will send that text for sentiment analysis, entity analysis, syntax analysis, and entity sentiment analysis, and classify the content. This will help us understand the mood and type of content. In this chapter, we are only going to display the response from the Cloud Natural Language API and not act on the results.

The topics covered are:

- What is the Cloud Natural Language API?
- Exploring the Cloud Natural Language API
- Integrating the Cloud Natural Language API with *SmartExchange*

Cloud Natural Language API

The Google Cloud Speech API is one of the machine learning services exposed under the Cloud AI vertical. This service is used to detect the structure and meaning of a text using machine learning.

This service does the following things:

- Helps us extract insights from the text; the text can be an email, a tweet, or a support request
- Supports content analysis for various languages
- Classifies the text and can provide a relation graph between texts
- Uses Google's deep learning models to predict as well as continuously improve the accuracy of the predictions

Some of the key features are as follows:

- Syntax analysis
- Entity recognition
- Sentiment analysis
- Content classification
- Multi-language support

This service can be used in combination with another service, such as the Cloud Speech API, where an audio file can be uploaded to the Speech API and the response text can be fed into the Natural Language API to perform syntax, entity, or sentiment analysis. Alternatively, using the Cloud Vision OCR (Optical Content Recognition) API, we can convert an image to text and then perform classification or entity analysis to gain more insights to the image.

The above use cases only scrape the surface of the power of the Cloud AI provided by Google. These services are only limited by our imagination.

Pricing

The pricing for this service is as follows:

Feature	Pricing
Entity analysis	Free till first 5,000 units and $1.00 per 1,000 units till 1 million units
Sentiment analysis	Free till first 5,000 units and $1.00 per 1,000 units till 1 million units
Syntax analysis	Free till first 5,000 units and $0.50 per 1,000 units till 1 million units
Entity sentiment analysis	Free till first 5,000 units and $2.00 per 1,000 units till 1 million units
Content classification	Free till first 30,000 units and $2.00 per 1,000 units till 250,000 units

You can read more about pricing here: `https://cloud.google.com/natural-language/` `#natural-language-api-pricing`. Now that we have the basics of the Cloud Natural Language API and understand the pricing model, let's get started with a hands-on exploration. Before we get started, we need to ensure that the required authentication and authorization is in place. In the next section we are going to look at that.

 When working with any Google Cloud AI service, we need to have either an API key or a service account key set up. Before we set up the API key or a service account, we need to have a Google Cloud project. If you already have a project, you can skip that section. Please refer to *Setting up an authentication* section from `Chapter 2`, *Setting Up a Smart Forum App*.

Enabling the API

Now that we have a project and we have both the API and service account keys, we will enable the required API and test our application. Navigate to the project home page (`https://console.cloud.google.com/home/dashboard?project=smart-exchange-b10882`). From the menu on the left-hand side, select **APIs & Services | Library**. Once we land on this page, search for **Cloud Natural Language API** and click on that card. Then, click on the **Enable** button. This will prompt you to set up billing, if you have not already done so. Once you have enabled the billing and the API, you should see that the Cloud Natural Language API is enabled:

In the next section, we are going to explore the API.

Exploring the Cloud Natural Language API

Please refer to the *Setting up the Rest Client* section of `Chapter 3`, *Cloud Vision API*, to set up a REST API client, either Postman or cURL, before you continue. Now that we have all the required setup done, let's get started with exploring the API. In this section, we are going to explore two APIs of the Cloud Natural Language API:

- Sentiment analysis
- Entity analysis

There are three more APIs that are offered as part of the Cloud Natural Language API, which are as follows:

- Syntax analysis
- Entity sentiment analysis
- Classifying content

While integrating with *SmartExchange*, we are going to make a request including all five features. But while working with Postman, we will be working with only two of them. We will start with sentiment analysis.

Sentiment analysis

Sentiment analysis helps us analyse the emotional opinion of the text, which helps us determine whether the attitude of the content's author is positive, negative, or neutral.

 Sentiment analysis doesn't tell us whether the author is angry or happy or sad, but it will tell us whether the content is positive, negative, neutral.

Request structure

We are going to make a request as follows:

Field	Value
HTTP method	POST
URL	https://language.googleapis.com/v1/documents:analyzeSentiment?key=API_KEY

| Request body | ```// SNIPP SNIPP
{
  "encodingType": "UTF8",
  "document":
  {
  "type": "PLAIN_TEXT",
  "content": "Enjoy your vacation!
  }
}
// SNIPP SNIPP``` |
|---|---|

In the above request, we are providing the content that needs to be analysed along with the encoding type.

Constructing the request

Now, using Postman, we are going to construct a request and fire it to the Cloud Natural Language API. Click on **New** and then **Request** inside Postman and provide a name as applicable. I have created a new collection named `Natural Language API` and placed this request inside that. You can import that collection into your Postman as well. This file is available in `Chapter 6\API\Postman folder`. Update the new request as follows:

Field	Value
HTTP method	POST
URL	`https://language.googleapis.com/v1/documents:analyzeSentiment?key=API_KEY`
Request body	```// SNIPP SNIPP
{
"encodingType": "UTF8",
"document":
{
"type": "PLAIN_TEXT",
"content": "Enjoy your vacation!"
}
}
// SNIPP SNIPP```

In the preceding fields, update the API as applicable.

Analyse response

Now, click on **Send** and we should see something like this in Postman:

As we can see from the preceding response, we have got the document sentiment with a magnitude of 0.9 and a score of 0.9. This is how we interpret the score and magnitude: Score is a value between −1.0 to +1.0, where −1.0 indicates a negative emotion and +1.0 indicates a positive emotion. 0.9 is closer to +1.0, which indicates that the overall document sentiment is positive, which is a given considering what the text is.

Magnitude indicates the overall strength of the emotion. It ranges from 0 to +infinity. Magnitude is affected by both positive and negative emotions in a text and longer sentences have greater magnitude. Apart from that, we have the sentiment analysis of each sentence in the text we are analysing. You can read more about interpreting sentiment analysis here: `https://cloud.google.com/natural-language/docs/basics#interpreting_sentiment_analysis_values`. We are now going to explore entity analysis.

Entity analysis

Entity analysis recognises common or proper nouns in our text and then tries to identify the entity associated with that entity, such as a person or the place of a thing.

Request structure

We are going to make a request as follows:

Field	Value
HTTP method	POST
URL	https://language.googleapis.com/v1/documents:analyzeEntities?key=API_KEY
Request body	```// SNIPP SNIPP
{
"encodingType": "UTF8",
"document":
{
"type": "PLAIN_TEXT",
"content": "President Obama is speaking at the White House."
}
}
// SNIPP SNIPP```

In the preceding request, we are providing the content that needs to be analyzed along with the encoding type.

Constructing the request

Now, using Postman, we are going to construct a request and fire it to the Cloud Natural Language API. Click on **New** and then **Request** inside Postman and provide a name as applicable. This file is available in Chapter 6\API\Postman folder. Update the new request as follows:

Field	Value
HTTP Method	POST
URL	https://language.googleapis.com/v1/documents:analyzeEntities?key=API_KEY

Request Body	```// SNIPP SNIPP
{
"encodingType": "UTF8",
"document":
{
"type": "PLAIN_TEXT",
"content": "President Obama is speaking at the White House."
}
}
// SNIPP SNIPP```

In the preceding fields, update the API as applicable.

Analyse response

Now, click on **Send** and we should see something like this in Postman:

As we can see from the preceding response, we got back a list of entities in the text we have sent. One was Obama and another one was the While House, and both of them got detected and the relevant metadata has been sent back to us on these entities. You can read more about entity analysis here: `https://cloud.google.com/natural-language/docs/basics#entity_analysis`. Similar to the the two APIs we have considered, you can explore the other three APIs as well. I have already created Postman requests for these and placed them inside the collection (in `Chapter 6\API\Postman` folder) for your convenience.

API reference

- You can find the reference for the sentiment analysis API here: `https://cloud.google.com/natural-language/docs/reference/rest/v1/documents/analyzeSentiment`.
- You can find the reference for the entity analysis API here: `https://cloud.google.com/natural-language/docs/reference/rest/v1/documents/analyzeEntities`.
- You can find the reference for the syntax analysis API here: `https://cloud.google.com/natural-language/docs/reference/rest/v1/documents/analyzeSyntax`.
- You can find the reference for the Entity sentiment analysis API here: `https://cloud.google.com/natural-language/docs/reference/rest/v1/documents/analyzeEntitySentiment`.
- You can find the reference for the classify text API here: `https://cloud.google.com/natural-language/docs/reference/rest/v1/documents/classifyText`.
- And finally a single API, using which we can invoke multiple APIs that are named annotateText: `https://cloud.google.com/natural-language/docs/reference/rest/v1/documents/annotateText`.

This is the API that we will be using in the *SmartExchange* app.

Integrating the Natural Language API with SmartExchange

Now that we have seen what can be done using the Natural Language API, let's actually integrate this into *SmartExchange*. We will allow the users to post a text response to a thread. Before we save this in the database, we will send the text for content analysis to the Natural Language API and get the analysis results. We are going to save the text as well as the analysis in our message collection and display the results to the user. The final output of the text analysis will appear as shown in the following screenshot:

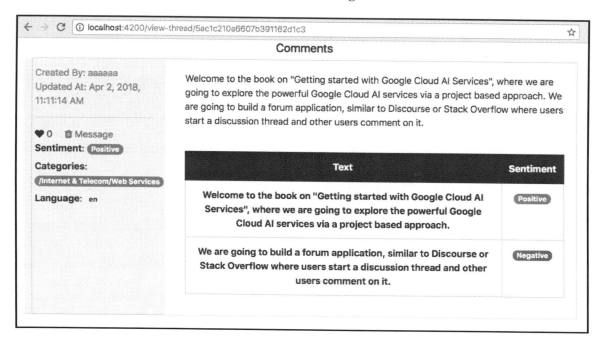

So, let's get started with the implementation.

Solution design

To achieve the preceding result, we are going to do the following:

1. On the view-thread page, the user is going to reply with a text message to the thread

2. The text will then be sent to the Cloud Natural Language API to be analyzed

3. The analyzed response, along with the text itself, will be saved to our database and the response will be sent back to the browser

4. The *Angular* app will process the response and update the thread

Setting up the server code

In Chapter 3, *Cloud Vision API*, I demonstrated how to use an API key to make a HTTP request from our Node.js application, and in Chapter 4, *Video Intelligence API*, and Chapter 5, *Cloud Speech API*, I demonstrated how to work with the client library. We are going to continue using the client library for this section, and the next as well. We have seen how to work with these using Postman; the same can be replicated in any language.

One awesome feature of Postman is that it can convert a HTTP request to any programming language. Once we have validated a HTTP request, we can click on the Code link present just below the button to Send and Save the request. This will show a popup and a language selection, and the code for that language can be generated on the fly, as shown in the following screenshot:

Simple and easy, isn't it?

To continue development, make sure you are working on the latest code or get a copy from `https://github.com/PacktPublishing/Getting-Started-with-Google-Cloud-AI-S ervices` and then install the required dependencies by running:

```
$ npm install
or
$ yarn install
```

Installing dependencies

We are going to install only one dependency; `@google-cloud/language` (`https://www. npmjs.com/package/@google-cloud/language`). This will interface with the Natural Language API. Run the following command from the root of the application:

```
$ npm install --save @google-cloud/language
```

Alternatively, run the following:

```
$ yarn add @google-cloud/language
```

Defining routes

Now that we have the required dependencies, we will update the routes. To work with the Natural Language API, we are going to add only one route that will accept the text and respond back with the Natural Language response. Update `server\routes\cloud-ai-api.ts` and add the upload-audio route as shown in the following code:

```
// SNIPP SNIPP
router.post('/upload-image/:threadId', Authenticate, Authorize('user'),
upload.single('image-reply'), cloudAIAPI.uploadImage);
router.post('/upload-video/:threadId', Authenticate, Authorize('user'),
upload.single('video-reply'), cloudAIAPI.uploadVideo);\
router.post('/upload-audio/:threadId', Authenticate, Authorize('user'),
upload.single('audio-reply'), cloudAIAPI.uploadAudio);
router.post('/post-message', Authenticate, Authorize('user'),
cloudAIAPI.postMessage);
// SNIPP SNIPP
```

Updating the message model

Next, we are going to update our message model. We are going to save categories, documentSentiment, entities, sentences, tokens, and language. Update `server\models\message.ts` as shown in the following code:

```
// SNIPP SNIPP
nlpCategories: [{
    type: Schema.Types.Mixed,
    default: []
}],
nlpDocumentSentiment: {
    type: Schema.Types.Mixed
},
nlpEntities: [{
    type: Schema.Types.Mixed,
    default: []
}],
nlpSentences: [{
    type: Schema.Types.Mixed,
    default: []
}],
nlpTokens: [{
    type: Schema.Types.Mixed,
    default: []
}],
nlpLanguage: String
// SNIPP SNIPP
```

Updating the controller

Now that we are done defining the routes and updating the model, we will work on the logic, as discussed in the *Solution design* section. We are going to add a new method to CloudAIAPI class named `postMessage`. Open `server\controllers\cloud-ai-api.ts`, where we will first add the required `imports` and `LanguageServiceClient`. Before the class definition, add the following code:

```
// SNIPP SNIPP
const language = require('@google-cloud/language');
const nlpClient = new language.LanguageServiceClient({
    credentials: JSON.parse(process.env.GCP_SK_CREDENTIALS)
});
// SNIPP SNIPP
```

Using the environment variable we have set in the .env file, we are using a GCP_SK_CREDENTIALS value to initialise a new LanguageServiceClient. Next, we are going to create a new method named postMessage, which will read the request body as the base message:

```
// SNIPP SNIPP
postMessage = (req, res) => {
 let message = req.body;
 message.createdBy = req.user;
 message.lastUpdatedBy = req.user;
}
// SNIPP SNIPP
```

Then, we will pass the description to the Natural Language API and get a response:

```
// SNIPP
const request = {
    encodingType: 'UTF8',
    document: {
        content: message.description,
        type: 'PLAIN_TEXT'
    },
    features: {
        extractSyntax: true,
        extractEntities: true,
        extractDocumentSentiment: true,
        extractEntitySentiment: true,
        classifyText: true
    }
}
nlpClient.annotateText(request)
    .then(results => {
        // CODE BELOW
    })
    .catch(err => {
        console.error('ERROR:', err);
        return res.status(500).json(err);
    });
// SNIPP
```

Next, we are going to save the response to the database along with the message:

```
// SNIPP
results = results[0];
msg.nlpCategories = results.categories;
msg.nlpTokens = results.tokens;
msg.nlpEntities = results.entities;
```

```
msg.nlpDocumentSentiment = results.documentSentiment;
msg.nlpLanguage = results.language;
msg.nlpSentences = results.sentences;
let message = new Message(msg);

message.save((err, msg) => {
    if (err) {
        console.log(err);
        return this.respondErrorMessage(res, err);
    }
    res.status(200).json(msg);
});
// SNIPP
```

This wraps up our controller logic as well as our service-side logic. In the next section, we are going work on the client-side logic.

Setting up the client code

We will continue from where we left off in Chapter 5, *Cloud Speech API*. Since we have already set up all the needed dependencies, we will continue with the development. We are only going to make two changes on the client side:

- Update the message POST API URL to the new one we have created
- Update the view thread component to display the result

Updating the POST API URL

In client\app\services\message.service.ts, we are going to update addMessage() as follows:

```
// SNIPP SNIPP
addMessage(message: Message): Observable < Message > {
  return this.http.post < Message > ('/api/post-message', message);
}
// SNIPP SNIPP
```

We have updated the end point to which we have posted the message.

Updating the view thread component

We are going to update `client\app\view-thread\view-thread.component.html` by adding the relevant response information. Add the following snippet after we display the segment `LabelAnnotations`:

```
// SNIPP SNIPP
<!-- Sentiment -->
<div *ngIf="message.nlpDocumentSentiment">
 <b>Sentiment</b>:
 <label class="badge badge-pill badge-success"
*ngIf="message.nlpDocumentSentiment.score > 0.1">
 Positive
 </label>
 <label class="badge badge-pill badge-info"
*ngIf="message.nlpDocumentSentiment.score === 0">
 Neutral
 </label>
 <label class="badge badge-pill badge-danger"
*ngIf="message.nlpDocumentSentiment.score < 0.1">
 Negative
 </label>
</div>
<!-- Catgories -->
<div *ngIf="message.nlpCategories.length > 0">
 <b>Categories</b>:
 <label class="badge badge-pill badge-info" *ngFor="let c of
message.nlpCategories">
 {{c.name}}
 </label>
</div>
<!-- Language -->
<div *ngIf="message.nlpLanguage">
 <b>Language</b>:
 <label class="badge badge-pill badge-default">
 {{message.nlpLanguage}}
 </label>
</div>
// SNIPP SNIPP
```

Next, add the following snippet after the transcriptions table:

```
// SNIPP SNIPP
<div class="table-responsive" *ngIf="message.nlpSentences.length > 0">
 <table class="table table-bordered">
 <thead class="thead-dark text-center">
 <tr>
```

```
<th scope="col">Text</th>
<th scope="col">Sentiment</th>
</tr>
</thead>
<tbody>
<tr class="text-center" *ngFor="let s of message.nlpSentences">
<th>
{{s.text.content}}
</th>
<th>
<label class="badge badge-pill badge-success" *ngIf="s.sentiment.score >
0.1">
 Positive
</label>
<label class="badge badge-pill badge-info" *ngIf="s.sentiment.score ===
0">
 Neutral
</label>
<label class="badge badge-pill badge-danger" *ngIf="s.sentiment.score <
0.1">
 Negative
</label>
</th>
</tr>
</tbody>
</table>
</div>
// SNIPP SNIPP
```

Save all the files to continue, and we are ready to test.

Testing the app

To test the app, from the root of the application folder, run the following:

```
$ npm run dev
```

Alternatively, run this:

```
$ yarn dev
```

Either of these will launch our application. From the home page, click on **Create Thread** and create a new thread named NLP API Test or any name as you please. Once we create a new thread, navigate to the view thread page. Add a text response and click on the **Reply** button. This will upload the message contents to our server and then to the Cloud Natural Language API.

Once we get the response, we save that along with the other content in our database and respond with the newly created message. And this is how the final message should look:

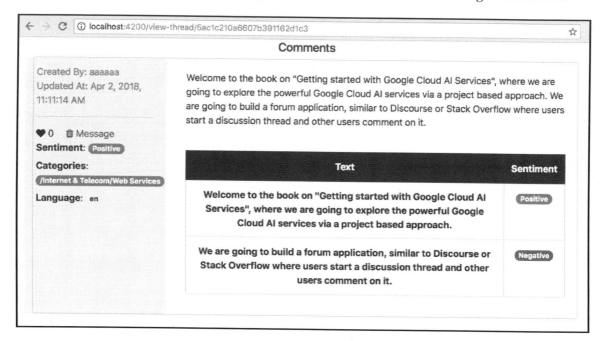

You can try with various text replies and test the complete flow end to end.

 Keep an eye on the number of API requests you are making to the Natural Language API.

To wrap up this chapter, we are going to push the code to Heroku.

Deploying to Heroku

This step is optional and you can do it if you are interested in deploying this app to Heroku. To continue with this section, you need to have set up a Heroku account and installed the Heroku Toolbelt. Once that is done, open a new Command Prompt or Terminal inside the `smart-exchange-base` folder. Run the following:

```
$ heroku login
```

This will prompt you for the Heroku credentials that you have signed up with. Next, let's get our application ready for deployment. Run the following:

```
$ npm run build
```

Alternatively, run this:

```
$ yarn build
```

Either of these will run the required scripts to build the final `dist` folder, which will be deployed to Heroku. Once the build is completed, run the following:

```
$ git add -A
$ git commit -am "Cloud Natural language API Integration Commit"
```

Let's, push the code to Heroku. Run the following:

```
$ git push heroku master
```

If everything goes well, the code will be uploaded to Heroku and you should be able to view the application at `https://smart-exchange.herokuapp.com`.

Summary

In this chapter, we have gone through the Google Natural Language API and we have worked with the annotateText API. We also set up the code that is required for integrating this API with the *SmartExchange* app. In the next chapter, we are going to work with the Cloud Translation API.

Cloud Translation 7

In the last chapter, we saw how to work with Cloud Natural Language API and how we can integrate the Cloud Natural Language API with *SmartExchange* to detect emotion in text. In this chapter, we are going to work with Cloud Translation API. Next to each text reply, we are going to provide a button, using which the message text can be converted to any language the user prefers.

The topics covered in this chapter are:

- What is Cloud Translation API?
- Exploring Translation API
- Integrating Translation API with *SmartExchange*

Cloud Translation API

Google Cloud Speech API is one of the machine learning services exposed under the Cloud AI vertical. This service is used to translate text from one language to another using state-of-the-art **Neural Machine Translation** (**NMT**).

This service offers the following:

- Provides an on-the-fly translation service, from a sentence to a document
- Can support up to 104 languages, as of this writing
- Can detect language in source text automatically
- Is highly scalable and affordable
- Continuously updates from various sources and provides us the best translation service

Pricing

The pricing for this service is as follows:

Feature	Pricing
Text translation	$20 for first 1 million characters a month
Language detection	$20 for first 1 million characters a month

You can read more about pricing here: `https://cloud.google.com/translate#cloud-translation-api-pricing`. Now that we have the basics of the Cloud Translation API and understand the pricing model, let's get started with a hands-on exploration. Before we get started, we need to set up the required authentication and authorization. In the next section, we are going to look at that.

 When working with any Google Cloud AI service, we need to have either an API key or a service account key set up. Before we set up the API key or a service account, we need to have a Google Cloud project. If you already have a project, you can skip that section. Please refer to *Setting up an authentication* section from `Chapter 2`, *Setting Up a Smart Forum App.*

Enabling API

Now that we have a project and we have both API and service account keys, we will enable the required API and test our application. Follow these steps to enable the API:

1. Navigate to the project home page (`https://console.cloud.google.com/home/dashboard?project=smart-exchange-b10882`). From the menu on the left-hand side, select **APIs & Services | Library**.
2. Once we land on this page, search for **Google Cloud Translation API** and click on that card.
3. Then, click on the **Enable** button. This will prompt you to set up billing, if you have not already done so.
4. Once you have enabled the billing and the API, you should see that the Cloud Natural Language API is enabled on your screen.

In the next section, we are going to explore the API.

Exploring Cloud Translation API

Please refer to the *Setting up a Rest Client* section from `Chapter 3`, *Cloud Vision API* to set up a REST API client, either Postman or cURL before you continue. Now that we have all the required setup done, let's get started with exploring the API.

In this section, we are going to explore two APIs of Cloud Translation:

- Discovering supporting languages
- Translating text

Apart from this, there is another API, which helps us discover the language of the text. While integrating with *SmartExchange*, we are going to make a request to the supporting languages API and then make a request to translate text, to get the translated text. We will start with discovering supporting languages.

Discovering supporting languages

This API returns a list of supported languages that the translate API can work on. We are going to use the response from this API to show users a list of supported languages that a user can convert this document to.

Request structure

We are going to make a request as follows:

Field	Value
HTTP method	POST
URL	https://translation.googleapis.com/language/translate/v2/languages?key=API_KEY

Request body	`// SNIPP SNIPP`
	`{`
	`  "target": "en"`
	`}`
	`// SNIPP SNIPP`

In the previous payload, we are providing the target language in which the list of names should be returned. For instance, if we provide *en*, we will receive the response in English; *fr* will return French. You can explore this while playing with the API.

Constructing the request

Now, using Postman, we are going to construct a request and fire it to the Cloud Translation API using these steps:

1. Click on **New** and then **Request** inside **Postman**, and provide a name as applicable. I have created a new collection named `Cloud Translation API` and placed this request inside that. You can import that collection into your Postman as well. This file is available in the `Chapter 7\API\Postman` folder.

2. Update the new request as follows:

Field	Value
HTTP method	POST
URL	https://translation.googleapis.com/language/translate/v2/languages?key=API_KEY

Request body	// SNIPP SNIPP
	{
	  "target": "en"
	}
	// SNIPP SNIPP

In the previous fields, update the API key as applicable.

Analysing response

Now then we have the request constructed, click on **Send.** We should see something like this in Postman:

As we can see from the response, we get the language code and the name of language in the target language we have specified while making the request. You can change the target language to **zh** or **fr** and so on, and see the response. You can read more about language support here: `https://cloud.google.com/translate/docs/languages`. Next, we are going to explore text translation API.

Text translation

Text translation API helps us convert a piece of text to a target language that it supports. The translation happens through the **Neural Machine Translation (NMT)** model. If the NMT is not supported for any language translation pair, then **Phrase Based Machine Translation (PBMT)** is used.

Request structure

We are going to make a request as follows:

Field	Value
HTTP method	POST
URL	https://translation.googleapis.com/language/translate/v2?key=API_KEY

Request body	`// SNIPP SNIPP`
	`{`
	`  "target": "fr",`
	`  "q": "Hello World!"`
	`}`
	`// SNIPP SNIPP`

In the previous request, we are providing the text that we want to translate to and the target language.

 Do note that the source language need not be English alone.

Constructing the request

Now, using Postman, we are going to construct a request and fire it to the Cloud Translation API. Click on **New** and then **Request** inside Postman and provide a name as applicable. This file is available in the `Chapter 7\API\Postman` folder.

Update the new request as follows:

Field	Value
HTTP method	POST
URL	https://translation.googleapis.com/language/translate/v2?key=API_KEY

Request body	```
	// SNIPP SNIPP
	{
	 "target": "fr",
	 "q": "Hello World!"
	}
	// SNIPP SNIPP
	``

In the previous fields, update the API key as applicable.

Analyse response

Now click on **Send** and we should see something like this in Postman:

As we can see from the previous response, the text is converted from English to French. You can read more about the translate API here: https://cloud.google.com/translate/docs/translating-text.

Similar to this, you can explore the language detection API: `https://cloud.google.com/translate/docs/detecting-language`.

You can find the reference for Discovering Supporting Languages API here: `https://cloud.google.com/translate/docs/reference/languages`. You can find the reference for Translate API here: `https://cloud.google.com/translate/docs/reference/translate`. You can find the reference for Language Detection API here: `https://cloud.google.com/translate/docs/reference/detect`.

Integrating Translate API with SmartExchange

Now that we have seen what can be done using Translate API, let's actually integrate this into *SmartExchange*. Next to every text message, we are going have a **translate** button. When the user clicks on the button, we show a popup with the Message text and a dropdown to pick the target language to translate this message to. Once we have successfully translated it, we are going to show the translated text in the same popup. The final output of the text analysis will look as shown here:

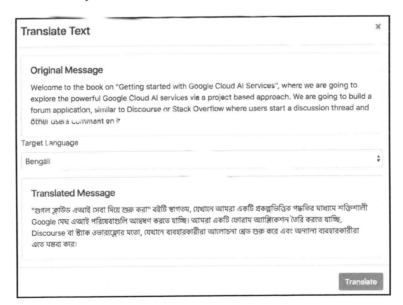

So, let's get started with the implementation.

Solution design

To achieve our solution, we are going to do the following:

1. On the view-thread page, the user is going see a **Translate** button.
2. Clicking on the translate button, we show a popup where the user selects the target language.
3. When then send the target language and the message to the Cloud Translation API and get the response.
4. We then tag the response against the language and save the entire message to the database, so, from the next time onwards, we can reply from DB instead of making an API call. The persisted response will then be sent back to the browser.
5. The *Angular* app will process the response and update the thread.

Setting up the server code

To get started, make sure you are working on the latest code or get a copy from `https://github.com/PacktPublishing/Getting-Started-with-Google-Cloud-AI-Services` and then install the required dependencies by running the following:

```
$ npm install
or
$ yarn install
```

Once this is done, we will proceed further. In this chapter, we are going to use the `Node.js` client library for interacting with the translation API.

Installing dependencies

We are going to install only one dependency, `@google-cloud/translate` (`https://www.npmjs.com/package/@google-cloud/translate`), to interface with the Translation API. Run this command from the root of the application:

```
$ npm install --save @google-cloud/translate
or
$ yarn add @google-cloud/translate
```

Defining routes

Now that we have the required dependencies, we will update the routes. To work with Translation API, we are going to add two routes. One will return the list of supported languages and the other will translate text. Update `server\routes\cloud-ai-api.ts` and add the supported-languages and translate-message routes as shown here:

```
// SNIPP SNIPP
router.get('/supported-languages', Authenticate, Authorize('user'),
cloudAIAPI.getSupportedLanguages);
router.post('/translate-message', Authenticate, Authorize('user'),
cloudAIAPI.translateMessage);
// SNIPP SNIPP
```

Updating the message model

Next, we are going to update our message model. We are going to save the translated text, along with the language code to our message. This way, we can retrieve the translation for a given message and not hit the Translate API every time. Update `server\models\message.ts` as shown here:

```
// SNIPP SNIPP
translations: {
    type: Schema.Types.Mixed
}
// SNIPP SNIPP
```

Do note that this variable stores an object and not an array. The object will be built as follows:

```
// SNIPP SNIPP
{
 'fr': 'Bonjour le monde!',
 'en': 'Hello World!'
}
// SNIPP SNIPP
```

So, querying this variable will be easy given the language code.

Updating the controller

Now that are done with defining the routes and updating the model, we will work on the logic discussed in the *Solution design* section earlier. We are going to add two new methods to CloudAIAPI, named `getSupportedLanguages` and `translateMessage`. Open `server\controllers\cloud-ai-api.ts` and we will first add the required `imports` and `LanguageServiceClient`. Before the class definition, add this code:

```
// SNIPP SNIPP
const Translate = require('@google-cloud/translate');
const translateClient = new Translate({
    credentials: JSON.parse(process.env.GCP_SK_CREDENTIALS)
});
// SNIPP SNIPP
```

Using the environment variable we have set in the `.env` file, we are using `GCP_SK_CREDENTIALS` value to initialize a new Translate client. Next, we are going to create a new method named `getSupportedLanguages`, which will return the list of supported languages from the Translate API:

```
// SNIPP SNIPP
SupportedLanguagesCache = [];
getSupportedLanguages = (req, res) => {
 if (this.SupportedLanguagesCache.length > 0) {
 return res.status(200).json(this.SupportedLanguagesCache);
 } else {
 translateClient
 .getLanguages()
 .then(results => {
 const languages = results[0];
 this.SupportedLanguagesCache = languages;
 return res.status(200).json(languages);
 })
 .catch(err => {
 console.error('ERROR:', err);
 return res.status(500).json(err);
 });
 }
}
// SNIPP SNIPP
```

We have a created a class variable named `SupportedLanguagesCache` where we are going to store the list of supported languages. For our example, we are not cache busting this variable. If you would like, you can have a scheduler/cron job run every 24 hours or 48 hours once and update this cache variable. This way, we can save quite a lot on the API calls.

Next, we are going to work on `translateMessage()`:

```
// SNIPP SNIPP
translateMessage = (req, res) => {
 let message = req.body;
 // let msgId = message._id;
 // delete message._id;
 let targetLang = req.params.target;
 translateClient
 .translate(message.description, targetLang)
 .then(results => {
 let translations = results[0];
 translations = Array.isArray(translations) ?
 translations :
 [translations];
 translations.forEach((translation, i) => {
 message.translations[targetLang] = translation;
 });
 Message.findOneAndUpdate({
 _id: message._id
 }, message, (err) => {
 if (err) {
 return this.respondErrorMessage(res, err);
 }
 return res.json(message);
 });
 })
 .catch(err => {
 console.error('ERROR:', err);
 return res.status(500).json(err);
 });
}
// SNIPP SNIPP
```

In `translateMessage()`, we `translate()` on `translateClient` and pass in the message description and `targetLang`. Once we get the response, we save that response on translations object and then send the message object back to the client. This wraps up our controller logic and our server-side logic. In the next section, we are going to work on the client-side logic.

Setting up the client code

We will continue from where we left off in Chapter 6, *Cloud Natural Language*. Since we have already set up all the needed dependencies, we will continue with the development.

Modifying the view thread component

I wanted to keep the translate feature simple. So, along with the existing text message, we are going to add a **Translate** button in the meta data column of the text message. Open `client\app\view-thread\view-thread.component.html` and after the `Delete message` section, add this code:

```
// SNIPP SNIPP
<!-- Any text message will have a nlpLanguage varible -->
<div *ngIf="message.nlpLanguage">
 <br>
 <button class="btn btn-info btn-block" type="button"
(click)="translateMessage(message)"><i class="fa fa-arrows-h"></i>
Translate Message</button>
</div>
// SNIPP SNIPP
```

Next, the required logic for `translateMessage` will be placed in `client\app\view-thread\view-thread.component.ts` and should be as shown here:

```
// SNIPP SNIPP
translateMessage(message: Message) {
 const modalRef = this.modal.open(TranslateMessageModal, {
 size: 'lg'
 });
 modalRef.componentInstance.message = message;
 modalRef.componentInstance.updateMessage.subscribe((msg) => {
 if (!msg) return;
 this.thread.messages.forEach((m) => {
 if (m._id === msg._id) {
 m = msg;
 }
 });
 });
}
// SNIPP SNIPP
```

Here, we are using the `NgbModal` instance to open translate message component, which we are going to create in a moment. Using the `componentInstance` on `modalRef`, we are sending the message to that component as input. Add this import to `client\app\view-thread\view-thread.component.ts`:

```
// SNIPP SNIPP
import { TranslateMessageModal } from './translate-message-modal/translate-message-modal';
// SNIPP SNIPP
```

Now we will create the translate message modal component.

Setting up the translate message modal component

Inside the `client\app\view-thread` folder, create another folder named `translate-message-modal`, and inside that, create two files named `translate-message-modal.html` and `translate-message-modal.ts`. Update `client\app/view-thread\translate-message-modal\translate-message-modal.html`, as shown here:

```html
// SNIPP SNIPP
<div class="modal-header">
 <h4 class="modal-title">Translate Text</h4>
 <button type="button" class="close" aria-label="Close"
(click)="activeModal.dismiss('x')">
 <span aria-hidden="true">&times;</span>
 </button>
</div>
<div class="modal-body">
 <div class="card">
 <div class="card-body">
 <h5 class="card-title">Original Message</h5> {{message.description}}
 </div>
 </div>
 <div class="form-group">
 <label>Target Language</label>
 <select class="form-control" (change)="onChange($event.target.value)">
 <option *ngFor="let l of languages" [value]="l.code">{{l.name}}</option>
 </select>
 </div>
 <div class="card" *ngIf="targetLang && message.translations[targetLang]">
 <div class="card-body">
 <h5 class="card-title">Translated Message</h5>
{{message.translations[targetLang]}}
 </div>
```

```
    </div>
    <ngb-alert type="danger" [dismissible]="false" *ngIf="error">
    <strong>Error!</strong> {{error.message || error}}
    </ngb-alert>
  </div>
  <div class="modal-footer">
    <i *ngIf="isProcessing" class="fa fa-circle-o-notch fa-spin fa-3x"></i>
    <button type="button" class="btn btn-success" [disabled]="isProcessing ||
!targetLang" (click)="translate()">Translate</button>
  </div>
// SNIPP SNIPP
```

Here, we have a select box, using which the user will select a language to which the text needs to be translated to. When the user clicks on the **Translate** button, we will make a request to the translate API to get the translated message. Apart from that, we have the required error messages and loading indicators. For the required logic, we will get started by adding the imports to `client\app/view-thread\translate-message-modal\translate-message-modal.ts`:

```
// SNIPP SNIPP
import { Component, Input, Output, EventEmitter, ViewChild, AfterViewInit }
from '@angular/core';
import { NgbActiveModal } from '@ng-bootstrap/ng-bootstrap';
import { ActivatedRoute } from '@angular/router';
import { TranslateAPIService } from '../../services/translate.api.service';
// SNIPP SNIPP
```

We are going to create the missing dependencies in a moment. Next, we are going to define the `TranslateMessageModal` component as shown here:

```
// SNIPP SNIPP
@Component({
  selector: 'sm-create-asset-modal',
  templateUrl: './translate-message-modal.html'
})
export class TranslateMessageModal {
  @Input() message; // fetch from view-thread page
  @Output() updateMessage = new EventEmitter < any > (); // Update the view-
thread component with updated message
  error: string = '';
  isProcessing: boolean = false;
  languages = [];
  targetLang = '';
}
// SNIPP SNIPP
```

The constructor will be as follows:

```
// SNIPP SNIPP
constructor(
 public activeModal: NgbActiveModal,
 public translateAPIService: TranslateAPIService,
 private route: ActivatedRoute
) {
 this.getSupportedLangs();
}
// SNIPP SNIPP
```

After the component has been initialized, we are going to fetch the list of supported languages. The logic for getSupportedLangs is as follows:

```
// SNIPP SNIPP
getSupportedLangs() {
 this.translateAPIService.getSupportedLanguages()
 .subscribe(data => {
 this.languages = data;
 this.languages.unshift({
 code: '',
 name: '--'
 });
 }, (err) => {
 console.error(err);
 })
}
// SNIPP SNIPP
```

When the DOM is finished initializing, we are going to make sure the translations property exists on the message. If we don't do this, we will face an error while working with messages that were created without the translations property:

```
// SNIPP SNIPP
ngOnInit() {
 this.message.translations = this.message.translations || {};
}
// SNIPP SNIPP
```

Next, we have the onchange event on the dropdown, where we update the class variable:

```
// SNIPP SNIPP
onChange(val) {
 this.targetLang = val;
}
// SNIPP SNIPP
```

Finally, here is the `translate()`:

```
// SNIPP SNIPP
translate() {
 this.isProcessing = true;
 this.error = '';
 this.translateAPIService
 .translateText(this.message, this.targetLang)
 .subscribe((data) => {
 this.message = data;
 this.updateMessage.emit(data);
 this.isProcessing = true;
 }, (err) => {
 console.error(err);
 this.isProcessing = false;
 this.error = err;
 });
}
// SNIPP SNIPP
```

In this method, we pass the target language and the message to the server to get the translated text, and then update the view-thread with the updated message. This concludes our translate message modal component. Before we proceed, we need to add this component to `client\app\app.module.ts`. First, let's import `TranslateMessageModal` into `client\app\app.module.ts`:

```
// SNIPP SNIPP
import { TranslateMessageModal } from './view-thread/translate-message-
modal/translate-message-modal';
// SNIPP SNIPP
```

Next, we will add this modal to `declarations` and `entryComponents`, as shown here:

```
// SNIPP SNIPP
declarations: [
        AppComponent,
        AboutComponent,
        RegisterComponent,
        LoginComponent,
        LogoutComponent,
        AccountComponent,
        AdminComponent,
        NotFoundComponent,
        HomeComponent,
        CreateThreadComponent,
        ViewThreadComponent,
        FilterThreadPipe,
```

```
        EditThreadComponent,
        UploadImageModal,
        UploadVideoModal,
        UploadAudioModal,
        TranslateMessageModal
    ],
    entryComponents: [
        UploadImageModal,
        UploadVideoModal,
        UploadAudioModal,
        TranslateMessageModal
    ],
// SNIPP SNIPP
```

Save all the files and we are good to move on.

Creating the Audio API service

To get the supported languages and translate text, we are using Translate API service. Let's create this service now. Inside the `client\app\services` folder, create a file named `translate.api.service.ts` and update it as shown here:

```
// SNIPP SNIPP
import { Injectable } from '@angular/core';
import { HttpClient } from '@angular/common/http';
import { Observable } from 'rxjs/Observable';
import { Message } from '../shared/models/message.model';

@Injectable()
export class TranslateAPIService {
  constructor(private http: HttpClient) {}
  getSupportedLanguages(): Observable < any > {
  return this.http.get < any > ('/api/supported-languages');
  }
  translateText(message: Message, targetLang: String): Observable < Message
> {
  return this.http.post < Message > (`/api/translate-message/${targetLang}`,
message);
  }
}
// SNIPP SNIPP
```

Finally, we need to add this service as a provider in `client\app\app.module.ts`. First, we will import `TranslateAPIService` into `client\app\app.module.ts`:

```
// SNIPP SNIPP
import { TranslateAPIService } from './services/translate.api.service';
// SNIPP SNIPP
```

We will also update the providers as shown here:

```
// SNIPP SNIPP
providers: [
 AuthService,
 AuthGuardLogin,
 AuthGuardAdmin,
 UserService,
 ThreadService,
 MessageService,
 VisionAPIService,
 VideoAPIService,
 AudioAPIService,
 TranslateAPIService,
 {
 provide: HTTP_INTERCEPTORS,
 useClass: TokenInterceptor,
 multi: true
 }
],
// SNIPP SNIPP
```

Save all the files to continue.

Testing the app

To test the app, from the root of the `application` folder, run this:

```
$ npm run dev
or
$ yarn dev
```

This will launch our application. From the home page, click on **Create Thread** and create a new thread named `Translate API Test` or any name you want. Once we create a new thread and navigate to the view thread page, we should see the translate button next to each text message:

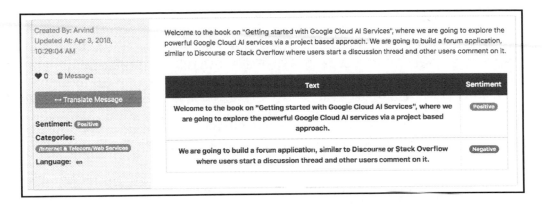

Next, when we click on the **Translate** button, we should see a popup where we see the original message and a selection for translated language. When we pick a language and click on **Translate**, we should see the translated message, as shown here:

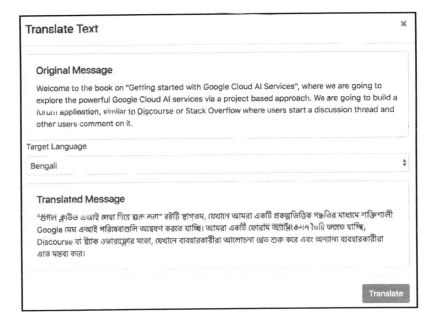

I have translated the text to Bengali.

Do note that this translation for this message will be saved in database. Next time, we are not going to make an API call but display from database.

In our application, we conveniently don't have an edit message feature. So, as long as the message is in our database, the translation is still valid. You can try other languages and test the complete flow end to end.

Keep an eye on the number of API requests you are making to Cloud Translate API.

To wrap up this chapter, we are going to push the code to Heroku.

Deploying to Heroku

This step is optional and you can do it if you are interested in deploying this app to Heroku. To continue with this section, you need to have set up a Heroku account and installed the Heroku Toolbelt. Once that is done, open a new Command Prompt or Terminal inside the `smart-exchange-base` folder, and then run:

```
$ heroku login
```

This is a prompt for your Heroku credentials that you have signed up with. Next, let's get our application ready for deployment. Run this:

```
$ npm run build
or
$ yarn build
```

This will run the required scripts to build the final `dist` folder, which will be deployed to Heroku. Once the build is completed, run the following:

```
$ git add -A
$ git commit -am "Cloud Translate API Integration Commit"
```

Let's push the code to Heroku. Run this:

```
$ git push heroku master
```

If everything goes well, the code will be uploaded to Heroku and you should be able to view the application at `https://smart-exchange.herokuapp.com`.

Summary

In this chapter, we went through the Google Cloud Translate API and worked with the language and translate API. Then, we set up the required code to integrate this API with *SmartExchange* app. This concludes our journey into Getting Started with Google AI Services. I hope you have learned the basics of Google Cloud AI and how to integrate it into any application.

Other Books You May Enjoy

If you enjoyed this book, you may be interested in these other books by Packt:

Google Cloud Platform Cookbook
Legorie Rajan PS

ISBN: 978-1-78829-199-6

- Host a Python application on Google Compute Engine
- Host an application using Google Cloud Functions
- Migrate a MySQL DB to Cloud Spanner
- Configure a network for a highly available application on GCP
- Learn simple image processing using Storage and Cloud Functions
- Automate security checks using Policy Scanner
- Understand tools for monitoring a production environment in GCP
- Learn to manage multiple projects using service accounts

Cloud Analytics with Google Cloud Platform
Sanket Thodge

ISBN: 978-1-78883-968-6

- Explore the basics of cloud analytics and the major cloud solutions
- Learn how organizations are using cloud analytics to improve the ROI
- Explore the design considerations while adopting cloud services
- Work with the ingestion and storage tools of GCP such as Cloud Pub/Sub
- Process your data with tools such as Cloud Dataproc, BigQuery, etc
- Over 70 GCP tools to build an analytics engine for cloud analytics
- Implement machine learning and other AI techniques on GCP

Leave a review - let other readers know what you think

Please share your thoughts on this book with others by leaving a review on the site that you bought it from. If you purchased the book from Amazon, please leave us an honest review on this book's Amazon page. This is vital so that other potential readers can see and use your unbiased opinion to make purchasing decisions, we can understand what our customers think about our products, and our authors can see your feedback on the title that they have worked with Packt to create. It will only take a few minutes of your time, but is valuable to other potential customers, our authors, and Packt. Thank you!

Index

Made in the USA
Lexington, KY
16 September 2018